NEW EDITI

C000272077

LEADER'S

SIMPLY | CHRISTIANITY

MANUAL

JOHN DICKSON

Simply Christianity: Leader's Manual
© John Dickson 1998
New edition 2003.

Matthias Media
(St Matthias Press Ltd ACN 067 558 365)
PO Box 225
Kingsford NSW 2032 Australia
Telephone: (02) 9663 1478; international: +61-2-9663-1478
Facsimile: (02) 9663 3265; international: +61-2-9663-3265
Email: info@matthiasmedia.com.au
Internet: www.matthiasmedia.com.au

Matthias Media (USA)
Telephone: 724 964 8152; international: +1-724-964-8152
Facsimile: 724 964 8166; international: +1-724-964-8166
Email: sales@matthiasmedia.com
Internet: www.matthiasmedia.com

The text of Luke was translated from the USB4 Greek New Testament by Tony Payne and John Dickson, with editorial assistance from Greg Clarke and Kirsten Birkett. © Matthias Media and John Dickson 2001

ISBN 978 1 876326 55 5

Cover design and typesetting by Lankshear Design Pty Ltd.

LEADER'S MANUAL

Table of Contents

Table of Contents (CONTINUED)

INTRODUCTION

There are an increasing number of courses designed to help the 'not-so-religious' discover the meaning and relevance of the Christian Faith today. As you'd expect, they each have their own particular style, emphases and usefulness. But one assumption lies behind all of them: that bringing the gospel to people in small groups (or one-on-one), in the context of ongoing relationships, is an enriching and effective experience. We are well aware that large public proclamation—at guest services, concerts and rallies—has an important place in the life and mission of the Christian community, but we are also aware that smaller, ongoing gospel ministry is often the more crucial component in our overall task.

Speaking personally, and as an 'evangelist' who spends a lot of time speaking at public events, there is nothing more enjoyable than having a group of people over to my house once a week for a month or so to learn about Jesus Christ. The questions, the interaction, the friendships, the humour and the good food all combine to make an extremely enriching ministry experience. More than that, to see members of the group—who have fast become friends—actually come to admire and love Jesus, is the most rewarding experience of all.

Simply Christianity is designed for just this sort of ministry. It is a five-part course based entirely on the Gospel of Luke. The goal of the course is to surprise and challenge ordinary people ('churched' or 'unchurched') with the unique story of Jesus Christ as told by Luke.

The methodology of the course is simple: let the Gospel tell the gospel! The course closely follows the outline and themes found in the Gospel of Luke. It begins with a study on the reliability of Luke (and the Bible generally) as a reporter of true events. Then, as Luke introduces us to Jesus, we are confronted with the surprising authority and power of Jesus—an authority and power that is unique in both its extent and its purpose. For we soon discover that Jesus' mission is not to conquer men and women with his great power, but to serve them. He has come to seek and to save the lost, to bring them back to their Creator. In the death and resurrection of Jesus, Luke brings his Gospel to a thrilling climax. Here we watch the powerful, authoritative Christ willingly sacrifice his life for a world loved by its Maker. We also watch him conquer death and rise to the right hand of God, from where he now offers the world his leadership and mercy.

In presenting this material, I have tried hard to let Luke tell the story his own way. This will hopefully mean that Christians of all denominational backgrounds will feel comfortable running the course for the people they have contact with. Within the parameters of Luke's Gospel, leaders will have the opportunity to raise the questions they want to raise, to answer the questions that arise in their special context, and to apply the material in a way that seems most fitting for their particular group of people.

A further benefit of Simply Christianity is the fact that the very successful *Jesus* video* is also based on Luke's Gospel. This means that segments from the video can be shown to supplement the Bible readings. In some cases, where literacy may be a problem, the video could even replace reading portions from the Gospel itself. Another obvious advantage is that *Simply Christianity* can function as very effective follow-up to an outreach strategy that uses the *Jesus* video.

This brings us to a brief word about how to actually get a *Simply Christianity* course up and running. Because the course functions quite well in a one-on-one setting, you could simply ask a friend if they wanted to know what you believe by doing a short five-part study. On the other hand, the course could be the more structured means of following up people who responded in some way to an outreach occasion.

Probably the most effective way of starting a course is to integrate it within an organized evangelistic program. That is, make the course the climax of a series of outreach events run over several weeks. At each event (church service, dinner, concert) encourage people who are curious to know more to join a short, informal course outlining the heart of Christianity.

The course was in fact developed in just this setting over a period of 18 months. The response was amazing. To those at St Clement's, Mosman, who supported this work, and to the many people who sat in my lounge-room, my warmest thanks.

In the following sections of this Leader's Manual, we'll be looking at how the course is put together, what it aims to do and how you can lead it.

I'd encourage you to take the time to read these sections carefully—they're not very long. I'd also be keen for you to pass on any feedback once you've run the course so we can make improvements in the future.

Thanks for your interest in *Simply Christianity*. I hope you find the experience of sharing the gospel of Jesus Christ in this way as rewarding and as enriching as I have.

John Dickson
Sydney, 2003.

John Dickson has a doctorate in ancient history and is a bestselling author in Australia and the UK. He is the author of several books on the Christian faith, including *Simply Christianity: A modern guide to the ancient faith*. He lives in Sydney, Australia, with his wife and three children, and is also an accomplished singer/songwriter.

Visit **www.matthiasmedia.com.au** for information about other books by John Dickson.

* Contact Matthias Media for details about how to get hold of the *Jesus* video. See page 2 for contact details.

ABOUT THE COURSE

1. The Values of the Course

Behind the course lie a number of important 'values' which influence the content, shape and usage of the material that follows. It is vital that each leader at least becomes acquainted with these values. Not everyone will agree with everything that follows, but a basic appreciation of these core values will make it a lot easier for the leader to remember, use and even modify the material in their own context.

a) Jesus and the gospel

There is a central principle to *Simply Christianity*, and it has to do with the nature of the gospel. The course is built on the assumption that to 'evangelize' means to declare the news about Jesus Christ. This may seem to be stating the obvious, but the implications of such a definition are far-reaching. It means that however much we may talk in the abstract about God, the problems of life, our sense of alienation, the reality of sin, the difference between grace and works, and so on, our evangelism is inadequate if it does not get past these things. It is not even adequate if Jesus is merely introduced at the crucial moment as the mechanism whereby God solves our problem. If the New Testament is anything to go by, our evangelism must be dominated by the proclamation of the event of Jesus and all that it means. The primary thrust of the gospel is how Jesus' life, death and resurrection prove him to be the saving Lord of the world, to whom we must give allegiance.

Maintaining this emphasis helps us to avoid a common pitfall, which is the potential for evangelism to become very 'me' centred. That is, it is easy to give the impression that the gospel primarily has to do with my great problem and what I have to do (or not do) in order to find the solution. Time and time again, however, the Bible speaks of the gospel as the 'gospel of God', the 'gospel of the Kingdom', or the 'gospel of Jesus Christ'. In other words, the gospel is primarily about what God has done to create his kingdom through Jesus' life, death and resurrection.

From start to finish, then, this course tries to focus on the life, death and resurrection of Jesus and how these events prove him to be the rightful Lord of our lives. Of course, ideas such as sin, judgement, atonement, grace and faith are by no means ignored. They are dealt with as they arise from Luke's presentation of Jesus. The motto of this course is simply stated: let the Gospel tell the gospel.

b) Relationship with the members of the group (or individual)

Of course, it almost goes without saying, but another reminder won't do any harm— relationship is vital to a successful gospel enterprise. The beauty of a course like this one, and many others like it, is that they are usually held in the home of the leader. This is an immediate sign to those attending that you are reasonably friendly. It takes the meeting out of the Evening Course pigeon hole (a very common preconception) and into the real world of human relationships. Not only does this aid people's enjoyment and reception of the course, it also hints at something about the nature of the gospel we are trying to communicate. It suggests something of God's openness to people.

Several factors will enhance this sense of relationship within the group, and most of them have to do with your hospitality as the leader. If you are warm and welcoming from the first moment, you will be sending a strong signal to everyone that they are not entering the 'Twilight Zone'. Also, the more food and drink you make available the better.

Food and drink have always been great ice-breakers, and gospel work is no exception. People do not expect to come to a course about Christianity and be greeted with good food and drink. They realise that they are entering the home of an otherwise normal, hospitable, friendly person, not a strict, wowserish, 'religious' type.

It is also important that when you finish the formal part of each meeting you encourage people to stay on chatting (and eating and drinking). In fact, it is worth treating the social time (before and after) as part of the course. This means making sure you have left enough time at the end of the meeting for this informal interaction to take place, especially if you are meeting at night. People often don't like to be out after 9pm on a weeknight.

If one of your group misses a session without telling you, make sure you phone to see if everything is OK with them. If they phone to pull out of a session because of sickness, make sure you also ring them back a couple of days later to see how they are doing.

Prayer is also part of our relationship with those to whom we bring the gospel. Praying for each individual member of your group once or twice a week is a good habit to get into.

Another good habit is writing to each member of your group personally at the conclusion of the course. At the end of the five weeks, it is worth just dropping each of them a quick personal note saying how much you enjoyed their company and participation. Also assure them that if they have any further questions or comments to make, you would be delighted to hear from them.

All this can get quite time-consuming, but that's gospel work!

c) Relaxed atmosphere

This, of course, is related to the previous point. Much of the atmosphere of a session will be determined by the friendliness and hospitality of the leader/host. However, there are some other things that can help.

Make sure that your house and living room (or wherever the meeting occurs) is clean and tidy. A messy place can set visitors on edge, let alone the leader or host.

Also, make sure there are enough comfy chairs to sit on. If anyone has to be uncomfortable, make sure it is you, or perhaps one of the other Christians (a trainee for example) in the group. It is great to have 14 people in a course learning about Jesus, but not if six of them are sitting on the floor, bar stools, or divan.

Another suggestion is to have music playing softly for the duration of the meeting.

If you were having friends over for dessert and coffee you would probably keep the CDs going. It doesn't distract the conversation. Depending on the kind of people you're expecting in your group, the same could apply. In fact, some music playing in the background can often fill that 'silent space' that can occur when a group of people who don't know each other gather for an hour or so. Just make sure it is appropriate music (i.e. the kind that your guests would enjoy) and that it is not too loud. It might be a good idea to avoid your collection of classic hymns.

d) Non-threatening

It is hard for us to imagine how nerve-racking it must be for a person to go into a stranger's home to investigate a topic as strange (to them) as Christianity. The nerves you will feel on the first evening of the first time you run this course are a helpful insight into half the terror in the minds of the members of your group as they knock on your front door for the first time. Anything you can do to set people at ease is a good thing.

For this reason, it is vital that a non-threatening and non-confronting approach is adopted in the running of this course. Several things can help.

Firstly, never ask a member of your group to read the Bible out loud. Quite a lot of Bible passages will be read out over the five weeks, and you (or a trainee) should do them all. Remember how you felt in school being asked to read out to the class? Reading the Bible for an adult is approximately as daunting.

Also, it is probably not wise to pray at the beginning or end of any session. Of course, you should pray before people arrive and after they leave, but there seems little point introducing people to the idea of chatting to the Creator when they are not even yet sure about chatting to you.

Another thing to avoid is asking any member of your group a directly religious question. It is fine to ask, "So Matt, what do you do with your time?" but not, "So Matt, what do you think Christianity is about?" or even, "So Matt, why did you decide to do this course?" If your group is getting on really well together, and seems comfortable in expressing their opinions about a wide range of subjects, you might ask questions of the group—such as the 'discussion starter' ideas that are listed in the leader's notes for each session. However, be sensitive to the group dynamics. Put yourself in your guests' position, and try not to embarrass them. In most groups I have run, I would not even ask a group member what they think a certain Bible passage means. Apart from making them feel undue pressure to wax eloquent on a topic they may have only thought about twice in their life, you may, in fact, get an unhelpful answer which you will then have to proceed to correct.

Speaking of unhelpful answers, another thing to watch for is how you correct any incorrect statements made by a member of your group. In general, it is probably best to allow 'heresy' to go unchecked. If a member of your group says, "Oh, I think all religions take you to the same truth about God", it is not absolutely essential you set them straight right away. This is especially important in the first few sessions, when you may not have had time to foster the trust and respect needed for a 'corrective' to take place. My suggestion is just to allow unhelpful comments to pass by the group. In the end, if the leader has done his or her job well, the group will respond far more to the material in the course than to the occasional erroneous comment from one of the members. Of course, if a member of the group is being decidedly antagonistic and unhelpful in their comments (a very, very rare thing in my experience), by all means gently respond with a few strong arguments. Remember though, in speaking to the 'heretic' you are also speaking to 5-10 others who are observing not only what you have to say, but how you say it.

These comments do not, however, apply to questions a member may ask you. So for example someone in the group may say, "Oh, I've always just assumed all religions taught essentially the same thing. Is that right?" In this case, by all means, answer as best you can. They have given you permission to correct them.

In the end, a non-threatening approach is often the most kind approach, and often the most successful too.

2. Overview of the Course

One of the beauties of restricting the course to Luke's Gospel is that by the end of the five weeks people really feel that they understand one whole book of the Bible. For the person who has never gone near a Bible (or at least not for a very long time) this makes God's word a less daunting and far more accessible book than they ever imagined. It is not uncommon, in my experience, for people to have finished reading the Gospel of Luke by the second or third week (even though their homework only requires them to reach the middle of Luke) and to have started on John of their own initiative.

This almost sole focus on the Gospel of Luke determines not only the content of the course, but also its overall structure. The Gospel of Luke falls into two parts. The first focuses on Jesus' authority and power as God's Messiah. The second tells how Jesus' Messianic authority is not used to conquer men and women, but to serve them by giving his life for their salvation. The hinge between these two sections falls in chapter 9, as the disciples (for the first time) realise and declare Jesus to be the Messiah. From that moment on, Jesus begins to explain to them that his role, as the Messiah, is to suffer, die and rise again. He sets his face towards Jerusalem and begins the journey towards his death and resurrection.

Based on this structure, the overall pattern of the course can be seen in the following table:

Session	Summary	Main ideas
1. Jesus, Now and Then	An introductory session focusing on the reliability of the Gospel record about Jesus' life.	• Christianity is unique among the religions in its focus on a person. It is not about ethics or philosophy or ritual. • Jesus' life is spoken of in various ancient documents (Josephus, Tacitus, Pliny, Suetonius). We know he lived, amazed people, died, and was reported to be raised from the dead. • The most comprehensive information about Jesus comes from the biographies (Gospels) of his life. We will look at Luke. • These biographies (and the Bible generally) are trustworthy. That is, documentary evidence is plentiful, it has not changed significantly over the years, and the writers are trustworthy.
2. In the Presence of Greatness (Luke 1–9)	A session devoted to explaining Jesus' authority as Christ.	• Images of Jesus through the years often emphasized his meekness/weakness—baby in a manger, blessing children, naked on a cross. Luke's biography begins with a significantly different emphasis. • The title 'Christ' essentially points to Jesus' right to speak and act powerfully on God's behalf. This is seen in the opening chapters of Luke's biography in terms of Jesus' authority to overcome evil, heal, forgive people's sins, control the environment and call on people to 'repent' and 'follow him'. • Even so, there are hints from the beginning that the power and greatness of this Messiah would be expressed in a way no-one expected.
3. Search and Rescue (Luke 10–19)	A session that explains Jesus' mission to seek and save the lost.	• At the moment the disciples finally confess Jesus to be 'the Christ', Jesus turns all their expectations about this ruler upside down. It turns out he has not come to conquer humanity with his power, but to serve humanity by seeking out the lost and bringing them back home to their Creator.
4. Jesus' Death (Luke 20–23)	A session emphasizing the meaning and importance of Jesus' death.	• The death of Jesus is a central event of the Christian Faith. What is its meaning? Jesus considered his death to be drinking the 'cup' of God's judgement. The crucifixion narrative itself also tells us that Jesus died so that access to God may be opened up (the tearing of the temple curtain).
5. Jesus, Here and Now (Luke 24)	A concluding session emphasizing the resurrection and describing what responding to Jesus means today.	• According to Jesus' own words, responding to him involved two things. • 'Repentance'—this is a change of attitude before it is a change of lifestyle. • 'Forgiveness'—all our wrongs are forgiven and forgotten. • People are urged to consider whether they have repented and asked for forgiveness.
Dinner	Though not officially part of the course, it is important to end each group with a pleasant social occasion.	• The benefits of ending with a dinner or some other social occasion are several. For starters, it is a good time for them to give back the Feedback Forms they were given as homework in the final session. More importantly, however, it sets the whole experience firmly in a relationship with you and the other members of the group. It also shows them that religion is not the only context in which you can relate to them.

3. A Typical Session

A typical session will fall into five parts:

a) Social

The session should begin with a healthy social component. Lots of food and drink make for a very comfortable environment. Remember, many of the people in your group will be very nervous about doing the course. Spending the first 20 minutes or so simply eating, drinking and chatting will help enormously. If you are more ambitious, and have the time and resources to do so, you could even start each session with a meal. This is great in terms of social interaction and building the relationships, but has real costs, both financial and in terms of the time each session takes. It might be difficult to have dinner, conduct the session, and still be finished at a reasonable hour.

b) Presentation

This, of course, is the focus of the night. Each presentation (by the leader) should take approximately 20-25 minutes. It can begin with a 'discussion starter' if you think your group is ready to handle it, but then the presentation is basically a talk which follows the Session Outline in each Guest's Manual. Personal stories and brief chit-chat are to be encouraged within this framework. Questions of clarification relating to the presentation should also be encouraged during this time. So, for instance, at the end of each subheading you may wish to ask, "Is that clear enough?" or "Any questions about that so far?" Basically, however, you should move through the presentation as smoothly as possible.

c) Questions

Questions about all manner of topics will occasionally arise, but, by having the official question time after the presentation, you are subconsciously encouraging questions that relate to Luke's portrait of Jesus and what it means for us. When you ask, "OK, are there any questions about the presentation, or about something you read in Luke's Gospel, or even about a related issue?" you should be aware that the first question is usually slow in coming. Give a few moments for that question to show itself, but if no questions come after 30 seconds or so, do not ask again or leave more silence.

On the issue of questions, it is vital that you are well-read. We recommend that you have at least read Leon Morris's commentary in the Tyndale series, to get a serious grasp on the Gospel of Luke and perhaps one of the apologetics resources recommended in 'Troubleshooting' later in this manual (pp. 18-19). It is an important responsibility of a leader to be knowledgeable and confident about the general topic. If you are slack in this regard, your group may be disappointed.

Having said this, it is not important that you appear to be an expert. There is no shame in saying, "I've not thought about that issue too much. Can I get back to you on that one?" If you are too 'brilliant' you may actually make people feel a little nervous about what they say in front of you and the rest of the group.

d) Wrap up

After the question time, a short wrap-up (of 3-4 minutes) is essential, especially when questions have wandered far afield. It focuses everyone's attention on the main point of the session. The wrap-up is also the time to advise people of the homework for the following week and what to look out for in Luke's Gospel in preparation for the following session.

e) Social

Finishing with more food, drink and conversation puts the whole session in the context of warm, developing friendships.

A s the leader of *Simply Christianity* you are performing the role of an 'evangelist'. That might be a scary thought if you've never actually seen yourself in that capacity, particularly if for you that word conjures up images of a loud, offensive, crowd-manipulating, pulpit-thumping preacher! But an 'evangelist', according to the New Testament, is simply someone whom Christ has gifted and given to a congregation to tell others about the gospel. The fact that you want to run a course like this, and that your church is keen for you to do so, is as good a sign as any that you are an evangelist.

But whatever you do, don't let the word 'evangelist' imply that it is your job to convert your hearers. It is not! The word literally means 'teller of the gospel' and doesn't carry the connotation of 'converter'. This distinction between 'teller' and 'converter' is important. If you go into a course feeling a pressure to convert people, you may actually find that your ability to clearly and naturally tell the news about Jesus is hindered. It is your job to tell; it is God's job to convince. To etch this in your mind, here's a tip. Before each session do two quick things: remind yourself that your role is simply to speak clearly and naturally about Jesus; and pray that God will open the hearts of the people in your group.

Having said this, you are still the most important person in the group (in terms of the success of the course). A good leader will nearly always make the difference between a bad course and a good one. Although you shouldn't feel pressure to convert people, you should feel pressure to explain things clearly. With this in mind, here are a few pieces of advice to help with the preparation and delivery of each session.

1. How to Prepare for each Session

Because clarity is the most important ingredient in your presentation, the key word for your preparation is 'familiarity'. Quite simply, the more familiar you are with the material of the course, the clearer and more natural your delivery will be.

In this Leader's Manual, you will find for each session a copy of the Session Outline (which is identical to what the Guests have in their Guest's Manual), followed by what we have called the 'Leader's Copy'. The Leader's Copy is an expanded version of the Session Outline, with suggested text for the leader to say, other information that might be useful, and tips about how to conduct the discussion. In the Leader's Copy, the text which corresponds to the Session Outline is printed in steely blue for easy reference. The rest of the text (in black) represents suggestions or instructions to you, the leader, about what to do and say next (e.g. "Give an opportunity for questions now").

The last thing you want to be doing is reading the Leader's Copy word for word to your group. It is only there as a full summary of the session. It does not represent the exact words you are to say. It simply fleshes out what should be said in your own words. It is also there as a memory prompt. However, if you have done the preparation, you shouldn't need to look at it during the presentation very much at all.

The Leader's Copy is not like the lines in a play. They are not your exact words for the group. By all means have it on your lap during the presentation, but don't read it. To help with your memory, there are a few things you can do.

After reading and re-reading the Leader's Copy, you might like to note down on the Session Outline in brief what needs to be said for each heading and subheading. This is mainly for memory practice, but you may actually find you would be more comfortable leading the presentation from your annotated copy of the Session Outline rather than flicking through the Leader's Copy.

After doing the above a few times you should be very comfortable with the material. I suggest you then get a highlighter pen and mark the key words on the Leader's Copy (that's if you decide to use it instead of your own annotated copy of the Outline). This will make it easier to glance down at your Leader's Copy and know exactly where you are and what needs to be said.

If you are used to giving presentations, either at work or in ministry, you may not need to fully rehearse each session—it depends on you. If, on the other hand, you have not had much experience doing this sort of thing, it is well worthwhile taking the time to give your presentation a dry run (or two or three). Just sit down in the place your group will meet (if convenient) and go for it. You'll probably feel silly doing it, but the benefits are well worth a few moments silliness. When you come to do the real thing, your presentation will be smoother, and your memory of the material greatly increased.

2. Tips on Doing the Presentation

A small talk

Basically, what you are doing in the presentation is a small talk. It is not a dialogue, discussion or debate. It is not like a weekly church Bible study either. Put crassly, the presentation is simply a 'monologue'. Although this word has bad connotations in some circles—'interactivity' is the preferred buzz-word—it has real benefits. Apart from keeping the session focused, the 'monologue' approach is far less confronting for people who have never been to a 'religious' group before. If you get them to read from the Bible or ask them comprehension or responsive questions, you are very likely to embarrass them or at least make them nervous. This will hinder the educational process.

Stories and examples

Like any small talk, giving examples and stories from everyday life helps the 'listenability'. I recommend that you occasionally (say twice a session) provide your own story about one of the items in the presentation. For example, in Session 3 you may give a simple testimony of how you first came to realise that Jesus wanted to seek and save people rather than just dominate them. Preferably, your story should illustrate the main idea(s) of the particular session. (Sometimes a good story wrongly placed and over-emphasized can make a presentation very confusing.) This means you will have to spend a bit of time thinking through the main ideas of each session and sifting through your memory to find something that will be a helpful example from your own life. Giving your own examples not only helps people keep interested, it also 'earths' the message of Jesus, showing how it applies to a real person day by day. But whatever you do, don't feel you have to go overboard with examples just to keep people's attention. One of the beauties of focusing on a Gospel is that you already have a pretty amazing story to begin with. If we can't make the life of Jesus sound interesting, we should probably 'stick to our day jobs'.

Clarify

To make sure your group is following what you're saying, it's a good idea to stop every now and then and ask if things are clear. Don't do it too often—say every couple of major headings in their Session Outline. And when you ask it, put the onus on yourself rather than them. In other words, don't say "Are you understanding this?", rather ask "Have I explained this clearly enough?"

Follow the Outline

Obviously, the Outline each member of the group has in front of them is only the 'bare-bones' of the full script you have on your lap. Because you will be saying so much more than what's on their Outline, they may at times feel unsure of where you are and whether they are following along properly. For this reason, it is important, firstly, that you are well aware of the bare content and structure of their Outlines. Secondly, you should make clear to the group when you are moving to a new heading or sub-heading on their Outlines. You needn't always say, "And now we are moving to point C". When you get to a new point, simply use the exact words of their Outline and say it with slightly more emphasis. They'll pick the cue.

Using the 'Jesus' video

Because *Simply Christianity* is based on Luke's Gospel, the popular *Jesus* video can be used at different points as a supplement to (or replacement for) the Bible readings. If your group does not have good literacy skills, this can really help the flow of each session. Even if literacy isn't a problem, the selective use of video clips can be a powerful way to supplement the presentation—for example, concluding your discussion of the significance of Jesus' death by playing the crucifixion scene from the video.

Of course, the leader needs to select and preview the relevant sections of the video, and have it ready to roll.

Another possible use of the *Jesus* video is to have copies available for group members to watch at home over the duration of the course. The shortened 80-minute version is very suitable for this, and provides excellent reinforcement of the passages and ideas that are covered in the course.

3. Follow-up

Anyone who has been involved in trying to reach people with the news of Jesus will know the prime importance of 'follow-up'. It is vital that you as a leader have a clear idea of how you will attempt to keep contact with those who have completed the course and would like to know more. The way you will know whether or not they want to know more is by the Feedback Form they return to you.

The most immediate thing you could do at the end of the five weeks is ask people if they would like to do a few more weeks looking at practical Christian living. You will find that many will respond in the affirmative. By the end of five weeks together it can be quite a sad thing for members of the group to disband. There are various sorts of follow-up that can be done—ranging from simply studying another book of the Bible (like Colossians or 1 John), to more structured courses such as *Just for Starters* and *Back to Basics* (from Matthias Media).

Having finished one such follow-up course you are still left with the dilemma of what to do with people who would like to do more. It is my suggestion that you start a new home Bible study group to cater for such people. Or, if you use an existing group, make sure that they are sensitive to the special needs of new and emerging Christians. To make this transition smooth, it is a good idea to invite the prospective Bible study leader to a dinner or social gathering that you organize at the end of the course. If they have the time you could even invite them to join the whole of the follow-up course. This means that there is a relationship already in place by the time they move into regular home groups.

In an ideal world, it would be preferable to invite a prospective leader to join the course from the very beginning of *Simply Christianity*. This consolidates the relationship, and will most likely ensure that more of the group move into a regular home group.

Apart from this 'formal' follow-up, you might also like to write a personal note to each member of your group in the week or two following the course. In the note you can warmly encourage them to keep pursuing their new-found knowledge of Jesus. Although very time-consuming, it is extremely valuable.

4. Training New Leaders

Success often breeds success. This means that if you run a couple of very positive *Simply Christianity* courses in your church, word will get out amongst the congregation that your groups are worth bringing friends to. In a very short time indeed you will find a need to have more groups. Unless you are willing to give up most nights of the week, it is a great idea to train others (more even than you currently need) to run the course. I learnt this the hard way. Turning inquirers away simply because I didn't have the foresight to train enough leaders was a very sad experience.

So how do you do it? The best way to train someone to run *Simply Christianity* is to let them sit in on the course, as if an inquirer themselves. By this I don't mean that they hide the fact that they are being trained from the rest of the group. I simply mean that the potential leader should just sit through a whole course once without assuming any leadership role at all (though they should take as many notes as they like).

In addition to this it is vital that you (the trainer) debrief the trainee leader after every session or two. The debriefing should involve a discussion of the course material itself, the ambience of the group, the most commonly asked questions, and any presentation tips you can recommend.

Ideally, the second stage of training should involve the trainee leader leading a group while you supervise. Admittedly, this makes the whole process slower but it will ensure a better result. Again, debriefing should occur after each session or two.

If this supervised option is not possible due to time constraints, it is even more important that the trainer meets with the trainee after each session. Even though you weren't there to see the trainee in action, they will still benefit from telling you what happened and hearing your suggestions.

5. Troubleshooting

The potential problems associated with running a course are many and varied. Here are some common ones:

Heresy

Every time you run a course you will hear from your group wild and wacky ideas and opinions about religion, UFO's, death, you name it. Generally, it is best just to let 'heresies' go unchecked. A 'corrective' may offend and it may distract the other members of the group. Unless the heresy is put to you as a question, don't bother tackling it.

Of course, there may be times (rare I should think) when a member appears to be pushing their strange views on the other members of the group. If this starts to happen it is advisable to do what you can to stop them, but of course, it has to be done with sincere gentleness.

Irrelevant questions

The question time is at times the best part of the course, especially if the questions flow directly out of the material. However, from time to time you will get a question that gets the group really interested but that in the long run is a serious distraction. You, as the leader, have to be the one to make the call on the importance of the question. Of course, you have to answer any sincere question, but you don't have to give a detailed answer to a trivial or distracting question.

Whatever you do, make sure you leave the wrap up until after the question time. It is vital that people leave the session with the story of Jesus buzzing in their heads, not the question of whether there is life on Jupiter.

Talkers

Every course will be made up of a variety of different people. In most groups of 5-10 people there is usually one who is a real 'talker'. It is important that they not take over the group. This may require some subtle redirections from time to time. It may at times demand that you speak to the person quietly after a session. You don't have to tell them to shut up, but you might just suggest that there are some in the group who might feel intimidated by how articulate they are.

Quiet people

At the other end of the scale, you may come across one or two people whose only words for the session are 'hello' and 'goodbye'. This is not so much a problem for you or the group, but it may indicate a problem for the person. I once had a similar situation, and it wasn't until the Feedback Form that this normally articulate and intelligent lady informed me that she felt overwhelmed by a couple of members of the group (particularly my trainee—there's another lesson to learn in that) who appeared to know so much. She didn't want to say anything in case she came across as religiously stupid. This was really my fault. I should have made more of an effort to quieten the 'know-alls' and talk with this woman after each session.

Tough questions

Many of the most trying moments for leaders come when they are asked difficult questions. The key to coping with such situations is to be prepared. Questions are of two types. The first are queries about the meaning of Luke's Gospel. Although Luke's main points are clear, there are intricacies in his detail that the leader must be fairly (though not exhaustively) aware of. The best way to prepare for these types of questions is to read through the Gospel of Luke slowly with a commentary at your side. Whenever you come across anything—and I mean anything—that you do not quite understand, turn to the commentary and see how it is explained.

The other questions are apologetic ones. These range from, 'Do dogs go to heaven?' to 'Why is homosexuality wrong?' It is advisable that you purchase a good apologetic book and read it thoroughly. In my experience, the most common questions have to do with the following issues:
  Suffering
  Other religions
  Homosexuality
  Feminism
  Jesus' deity
  Miracles
  Hell
  Demons

Some resources which are helpful in attacking these issues are:
  P. Barnett, *The Truth about Jesus* (Aquila Press, 1994)
  J. P. Moreland, *Scaling the Secular City* (Baker, 1987)
  J. W. Sire, *Chris Chrisman Goes to College* (IVP, 1993)
  C. Chapman, *Christianity on Trial* (Lion, 1988)
  So Many Questions (revised edition, Matthias Media, 2008), a video-based training
    course in how to respond to common questions.

6. Checklist

Have I rung to confirm all the participants?

Do I have the right number of Guest Manuals?

Have I set out the right number of chairs?

Have I decided where the best place is for me to sit?

Have I tested the video?

Have I prayed for these people?

Have I highlighted my Leader's Copy appropriately?

Have I got enough food and drink?

Have I turned the phone and answering machine down and the mobile phone off?

Is my house/room tidy?

Have I got my background music ready to go?

Is there enough toilet paper in the bathroom?

Have I run through the most likely questions for this study?

SESSION

1

JESUS, NOW AND THEN

1. 'Christ'-ianity

As the word suggests, 'Christianity' is all about a person, Jesus Christ. In fact, Christianity could be defined simply as 'responding appropriately to Jesus Christ'.

2. Information about Jesus?

a) Non-Christian Documents about Jesus
What they tell us about Jesus:

- when he lived
- where he lived
- that he was Jewish
- that he assumed the role of a public teacher
- that he attracted great crowds
- that he engaged in activities thought to be supernatural
- that he was executed; when and by whom
- that he had a brother called James who was subsequently executed
- that people claimed to have seen Jesus alive after his death
- that he was widely known by the prestigious Jewish title, 'the Christ'

b) The Biographies of Jesus' Life
- The Gospel of Matthew is famous for its lengthy record of Jesus' great ethical teachings.
- The Gospel of Mark is famous for its short, punchy style.
- The Gospel of Luke is famous for its emphasis on Jesus' friendship with 'non-religious' people.
- The Gospel of John is famous for its profound insight into the nature of Jesus.

Over the next five sessions, we will look at the Gospel of Luke.

3. Who was Luke?

- medical doctor, historian and intrepid traveller
- not an eyewitness to Jesus but a reporter of eyewitness accounts
- research began in the 50s AD; probably completed work some time between 70-80 AD
- highly educated Greek man

Luke's aim was to present the most accurate and relevant material on Jesus (read Luke 1:1-4).

4. The Big Idea

Christianity at its heart is not about rules or rituals but about a person, Jesus Christ —a person we can get to know through reading the Gospel of Luke.

5. At Home

For next week please read Luke 1-9 (or, if you run short of time, 4:14-5:39 and 7:36-9:22) and ask yourself: According to Luke, who is Jesus and what has he come to do? Note down anything you don't understand, or would like to discuss. We'll have a time for discussion next week.

Hand out Guest Manuals.

Begin with welcome and introductions. Perhaps just ask people to mention their names and how they spend most of their time. Suggestion: start with your co-leader or trainee and end with yourself. Then begin as follows...

- Let me begin by saying two important things about the nature of this course we're embarking on together:

  - First, I should make it clear up-front that this course does not focus on the teachings of a particular church or denomination but on those facts about Jesus Christ that Christians throughout the ages have agreed on. It is not therefore Anglican Christianity, Presbyterian Christianity, Roman Catholic Christianity or Baptist Christianity—it is 'simply' Christianity.
  - The second thing I should say is that the course has twin emphases. *On the one hand, the course is 'historical' in nature.* Hopefully that doesn't conjure up bad memories about school history classes. All I mean is that Christianity is about events that happened at a particular time and place; it is about a person who said and did certain things. In order to explore these things all these years later we need to do a bit of detective work with some very, very old writings, written almost two thousand years ago.

    On the other hand, the course is deliberately 'practical'. It tries constantly to answer questions such as: What do these old writings mean today?

What difference does Christian faith make in terms of one's perspective on life or day-to-day challenges?

- Are there any questions about the nature of the course...
- OK, let's begin with a working definition of Christianity...

1. 'Christ'-ianity

- At its heart Christianity is not a complex philosophical system like Buddhism, a code of morals like Islam, or a set of rituals as some Christian churches have presented it.
- The crucial starting point for this course is that...

As the word suggests, 'Christianity' is all about a person, Jesus Christ. In fact, Christianity could be defined simply as 'responding appropriately to Jesus Christ'.

- For some of us, this working definition may mean putting aside some of what we presumed Christianity was, and for the next five weeks just allowing this definition to be the starting point: "Responding appropriately to Jesus Christ."
- Since Christianity is all about Jesus Christ, the obvious point at which to begin our exploration of the man is to ask: What information have we got about Jesus?
- Our information about Jesus comes from a number of very ancient reports about his life. Some of these were written by people in the period who were not Christians; others were written by people in the period who clearly were Christians.

2. Information about Jesus?

a) Non-Christian Documents about Jesus

- If you're interested in reading the
  non-Christian references to Jesus from
  the period, the Extra Information for
  Session One contains a useful account
  of who wrote them and what they said.

  If you feel that your participants
  would be interested, turn to the Extra
  Information and read them one or two
  of these references. I would suggest
  Tacitus and the Talmud (see pp.30-34).

- For now, you might just be interested
  in a summary of what these 'non-
  Christian' reports tell us about the life
  of Jesus. It includes the following:

What they tell us about Jesus:
- when he lived
- where he lived
- that he was Jewish
- that he assumed the role of a public teacher
- that he attracted great crowds
- that he engaged in activities thought
  to be supernatural
- that he was executed; when and by whom
- that he had a brother called James
  who was subsequently executed
- that people claimed to have seen Jesus
  alive after his death
- that he was widely known by the
  prestigious Jewish title, 'the Christ'

- Clearly, these documents provide only
  the broadest outline of Jesus' life. They
  tell us little about what he was like,
  what he said to the crowds, what he
  felt life was all about, and hundreds
  of other questions people have been
  curious to ask over the years.
- For this kind of detail, we need to look at
  documents written by people with more
  than just a casual interest in Jesus. I am
  talking about the biographies of Jesus' life.

b) The Biographies of Jesus' Life

- Our detailed knowledge of Jesus comes
  from the ancient biographies of his life,
  called 'Gospels'. There are four of them:

The Gospel of Matthew is famous for its
lengthy record of Jesus' great ethical
teachings.

- Many of those great sayings you may
  have heard—'turn the other cheek';
  'blessed are the peacemakers'; 'our
  Father who art in Heaven'—come
  from Matthew's biography.

The Gospel of Mark is famous for its
short, punchy style.

- It is a brilliant read if you have about
  an hour to discover the meaning of
  the world's most influential man.

The Gospel of Luke is famous for its
emphasis on Jesus' friendship with
'non-religious' people.

- Here we read about Jesus castigating the
  hypocritical religious hierarchy of his
  day and yet welcoming prostitutes,
  enemy soldiers and 'secular' businessmen.

The Gospel of John is famous for its
profound insight into the nature of Jesus.

- Although the story is the same, the
  angle from which John comes at
  Jesus is quite amazing.

Over the next five sessions, we will look at the Gospel of Luke.

- The course is based on this biography partly because of its focus on Jesus' friendships with the 'not-so-religious'. This makes it the ideal read for anyone who feels religious matters are a little foreign. Although it is not as short as Mark's biography, there are still fewer words in Luke than in the sports lift-out in the weekend paper. For a book written almost 2000 years ago on the other side of the world, it is actually a very easy read.
- By the end of the course you'll be able to say that you have read one whole book of the Bible and know exactly what it says about Jesus. That puts you in the driver's seat, so to speak, in terms of being able to make an intelligent decision about the relevance of Christianity for your life.
- So, who was Luke? And where was he coming from?

3. Who was Luke?

- Luke, a medical doctor and historian, probably completed his biography some time between 70-80AD, though his research for the book began at a much earlier date.
- He had not personally known Christ but he had spoken with, and based his work on, those who had. In fact, several times during the 50s AD Luke had the privileged experience of travelling and working with one of the key eyewitnesses to Jesus' resurrection, a man known as the Apostle Paul. Paul wrote no fewer than 13 of the

other books in the New Testament. For Luke, this must have been a time of great inspiration as well as fruitful research for his own account of the life of Jesus.
- These experiences, combined with the fact that he was a man of high education —as indicated by the literary Greek of his biography—made him perfectly suited to produce a work of such importance.

- **medical doctor, historian and intrepid traveller**
- **not an eyewitness to Jesus but a reporter of eyewitness accounts**
- **research began in the 50s AD; probably completed work some time between 70-80 AD**
- **highly educated Greek man**

- But before we read the opening sentences of Luke's biography, where he tells us why and how he wrote the work, I should acknowledge that sometimes people have doubts about how reliable a book like this is. Some people ask: Can we trust what we read in this book? How do we know it hasn't changed over the years? How do we know Luke didn't just make the whole thing up?
- It's probably no surprise to learn that all of these questions have more than adequate answers—otherwise Christianity would have dried up years ago. But since not everyone is interested in such questions, the material dealing with these issues has been placed in the Extra Information section. Feel free to read it at your leisure.

Note to leader: If you have access to it and you feel your group would be interested, use material from the video presentation *Messages from the Memory Banks* at this point (available through your local Christian bookstore). Use the following introduction:

- Because this is a topic that requires a certain amount of expertise, it will sound better coming from experts in this field. We're now going to watch a short video that deals with this question of whether we can trust the ancient biographies of Jesus' life.

- For now it might be worth just reading the opening paragraph of Luke's Gospel.

Luke's aim was to present the most accurate and relevant material on Jesus (read Luke 1:1-4).

Note to leader: Before reading Luke 1:1-4 you may need to explain how to use the large bold heading to find the chapter, and the small number in the text to find the verse. Practise a couple throughout Luke, then read the opening paragraph.

Give an opportunity for questions now, then wrap up by reading out the 'Big Idea'.

4. The Big Idea

Christianity at its heart is not about rules or rituals but about a person, Jesus Christ—a person we can get to know through reading the Gospel of Luke.

- This first session may have felt a little weighted toward the 'historical' aspect of Christianity. I guess that's appropriate considering its the introduction to the topic.

- Let me conclude today/night by telling you how Christianity came to be part of my life and what difference it has made to me.

Leader should now spend 3-5 minutes (no longer) explaining how Christianity came to be (or remain) part of his/her life. Be sure to include practical examples of the difference Jesus makes in your life. In keeping with the whole point of session one, keep the focus of your story upon Jesus himself. Also, do not feel the need to explain the whole gospel through your story. You have four more weeks to do that. Just choose pertinent, 'introductory' themes which you feel will be helpful to group members.

If you have not told your story in any detail previously, refer to the following section, *Telling Your Story*.

Now advise participants of the homework.

5. At Home

For next week please read Luke 1–9 (or, if you run short of time, 4:14–5:39 and 7:36–9:22) and ask yourself: According to Luke, who is Jesus and what has he come to do? Note down anything you don't understand, or would like to discuss. We'll have a time for discussion next week.

- Thank you very much for coming; please stay for more food and drink, or feel free to go when you need to.

TELLING YOUR STORY

In the New Testament, the word 'testimony' usually refers to an official declaration about Jesus and his resurrection (usually by someone who witnessed the events), not the speaker's Christian life. For this reason, we will call a story of personal faith simply your 'story', not your 'testimony'.

1) Three Kinds Of Stories

a) ALWAYS A CHRISTIAN

Those who have been brought up knowing Christ have a unique story to tell. It won't be a dramatic 'before-and-after' epic but it will have its own appeal and power. The 'conversion'-style drama has actually become a bit of a cliché in our society so the 'always-a-Christian' story may in fact be more intriguing to many.

b) NOT ALWAYS A CHRISTIAN

As long as 'before-and-after' stories are not overstated, such accounts of conversion can be very useful in helping interested non-Christians picture what it is like to move from their own position to a Christian one.

c) RETURNED CHRISTIAN

Some believers were brought up loving God but turned their back on him for some time before returning with renewed faith. This type of story will have elements in common with both 'a' and 'b' above.

2) Why Use Your Story?

a) IT IS INTERESTING

On the whole people are interesting. A story of someone being or becoming 'religious' is an unusual and rare enough tale to keep the average person reasonably (if only briefly) attentive.

b) IT AVOIDS ARGUMENTS

Many people find it daunting to talk openly about 'God and stuff'. Your story of faith keeps the focus on something less scary—you! Furthermore, discussions about non-personal ideas (such as creation or hell) are easy to turn into arguments. Your own story, on the other hand, is pretty hard to argue with. People will rarely attack another person's personal experience.

c) IT IS EASY TO REMEMBER

Some of us find it hard to remember complete 'gospel outlines' and are worried about getting it 'right'. Telling your own story takes the pressure off a little. With a bit of practice most of us will be able to tell our own story in an accurate and engaging way.

3) Things To Avoid

a) FOCUSING ON 'SELF'

It is very easy to focus entirely on yourself and forget that what you're meant to be doing is explaining how you came to follow *Jesus*. Jesus should be the 'star' of your own story.

b) MISSING OUR DEEPEST NEED

It is also easy to turn our story into a tale of having our personal, psychological needs met by Jesus, as if Jesus were the 'great social worker in the sky'. In talking of the needs Jesus meets we should particularly mention our need for forgiveness of sins.

c) EMPHASIZING 'BEFORE'

Another easy mistake (for those with a 'not always a Christian' or 'returned Christian' story) is talking too much about 'before' and not enough about 'since'. Our emphasis should be not so much on our sinful journey before we knew God, but on the impact of God's grace on our lives since coming to know him.

d) EXAGGERATING

"Never let the facts get in the way of a good story", a famous cricketer once remarked. This should never be the case in our story of faith. Christ does not need our 'amazing' story to convince someone to be a Christian. Just tell it like it was and is! If you can make it funnier or more interesting, well and good, but do not stretch the truth.

4) What Makes A Good Story Of Faith?

a) PREPARE WHAT YOU WILL SAY

You don't want your story to sound 'rehearsed', but nor do you want it to sound confused. It is a good idea to work out the key moments and ideas that you want to convey.

b) TELL ACTUAL STORIES AND EVENTS

Most of us have particular occasions and people that had a big influence on our faith. Try to describe these in some detail so that your listener can picture you in that situation. The more they can picture you, the easier it will be for them to imagine themselves coming to believe in Christ. To give an example, instead of saying, "Someone explained that I needed forgiveness...", say something like, "I'd been invited to the home of my high school Scripture teacher and sitting in her beautiful, comfy lounge chair this middle-aged mum explained in a really simple way that I needed forgiveness..."

c) SPEAK NATURALLY

When an opportunity arises to speak to someone about your faith, it is all too easy to slip into 'evangelism mode'—the heart pounds, the five points of your gospel presentation race through your head, your voice speeds up and/or gets louder, etc! This is understandable, but to be avoided. When an occasion comes along, just take a slow, silent breath, say a quick 'Bless me Lord' (in your head), and speak naturally—as if you were telling a joke, a sports story, or something you saw on TV last night. The purpose of the welcome at the beginning of this Session was to illustrate the natural style in which stories from your life can be told. Speaking of your story of faith should be no different.

Exercise

1. On a piece of paper draw a timeline (from 0 to your current age) down the left-hand side of the page. Note down (in rough order) everything you can think of that contributed significantly to your present faith in Christ.
2. Now select the three or four most important points on the time-line and write down your story (using the above tips as a guide) on one A4 piece of paper (in note form if you wish).
3. Look for an opportunity to tell someone your story—a friend at church, a family member, or whomever—to gain more confidence in the way you present your material.

EXTRA INFORMATION
FOR SESSION ONE

Is the New Testament Trustworthy?

1. Non-Christian Writings about Jesus

Some years ago, just before Christmas day, a TV documentary series on the life of Christ was screened. Far from promoting the 'Christ' part of *Christ*mas, the show claimed to cast 'serious doubts' over the reliability of our knowledge about Jesus of Nazareth. One of the people interviewed on the program, a professor from a large German university, even stated that "Jesus probably never existed at all". The man sounded smart—German accents tend to do that—and he was a professor after all, so I was left with some questions: Is the Christian faith built on an invention or a myth? What and how do we know about Christ? Indeed, did he exist at all?

Only much later did I learn that the sceptical professor in the documentary was actually a professor of modern German literature. He was not a historian at all. He had a fancy title and was no doubt a highly intelligent man, but he was about as 'expert' on the question of the life of Christ as a professor of music would be on the existence of black holes. It turns out that the producers of the TV program had searched long and hard for a historian who would go on camera and deny the reality of Jesus' existence. When they couldn't find one they resorted to an 'expert' from another field, without letting the audience in on the secret. Since then I have discovered that finding a professional historian who denies the first century existence of Jesus Christ is about as difficult as finding a professional scientist who rejects the existence of DNA.

So then, historically speaking, how and what do we really know about the man Jesus Christ? Many, many books have been written on this topic so the following pages are offered only as a summary of some of the relevant points.

Our knowledge of the life of Jesus Christ derives mostly from ancient documents of two types: those written by non-Christians in the period shortly after Christ and those written by Christians. Of course, there are many more Christian texts than non-Christian ones, but this is to be expected, since obviously Christians were highly motivated to preserve the facts about their leader. To offer a modern parallel, I imagine more financial documents have been produced by economists this century than by rock musicians, and certainly more lyrics have been written by pop artists than by financiers!

Nevertheless, the few documents we have from non-Christian sources in the ancient period provide some interesting pieces of information about the life of Jesus. In fact, it may surprise you to know that the broad outline of Christ's life can be known from these references, without even turning to the Christian documents. Let me quote just four of the six references from antiquity.

Flavius Josephus, a Jewish historian writing around 80 AD, mentions Jesus on two separate occasions in his books. In his multi-volume work *The Antiquities of the Jews* (Book 18, chapter three) he writes about Jesus in the following way:

> Now about this time there lived a wise man called Jesus... Indeed, he was a man who performed startling feats. He was a teacher of the people... and he drew in many from among both the Jews and the Greeks. And those who were devoted to him from the start did not cease their devotion even after Governor Pilate, on the basis of charges laid against him by our leaders, condemned him to a cross. For [it is reported] he appeared to them alive again... And the group of 'Christians', named after him, has still not disappeared to this day.*

A little later in the work (Book 20, chapter nine), Josephus recounts the execution of one of Jesus' brothers (yes, Jesus had several younger brothers and sisters), and in so doing, again makes passing reference to Jesus:

> But this younger Ananus, who, as we have told you already, took the high priesthood, was a bold man in his temper, and very insolent... he assembled the Sanhedrin of judges, and brought before them the brother of Jesus whom they call the Christ, whose name was James, and some others, and when he had formed an accusation against them as breakers of the law, he delivered them to be stoned to death...

This text is fascinating for historians of early Christianity. The New Testament (the second half of the Bible) recounts a little about Jesus' brother, James. We know, for instance, that although he started out a sceptic about his famous brother's career, he ended up being one of the key early Christian leaders, claiming even to be an eyewitness to Jesus' resurrection. Our biblical information about James, however, cuts off with him still alive and well in Jerusalem, actively proclaiming the significance of Jesus. What Josephus writes completes the picture. Obviously, James' efforts to promote the message about his brother ran foul of the authorities and, just like his brother 25 years before, James found himself paying the supreme price of his own life.

Cornelius Tacitus is regarded as ancient Rome's greatest historian. His *Annals of Imperial Rome*, written shortly after Josephus (in 115 AD), are the basis of much of our most accurate information about Emperors Tiberius, Claudius, Nero, and many of the other famous figures of the period. In recounting the persecutions against the early Christians, Tacitus records the following about Jesus:

> Christians derived their name from a man called Christ, who, during the reign of Emperor Tiberius had been executed by sentence of the procurator Pontius Pilate. The deadly superstition, thus checked for the moment, broke out afresh not only in Judaea, the first source of the evil, but also in the City of Rome, where all things hideous and shameful from every part of the world meet and become popular.
>
> Cornelius Tacitus, *Annals of Imperial Rome* (25.44)

As you can tell from his comments, Tacitus was not exactly a 'fan' of Christ or of the early Christians. Yet as a matter of historical accuracy Tacitus feels it necessary to include a reference to Jesus and confirm some details about his execution—where, when and by whom. Though Tacitus provides no new information about Christ, it does confirm from the Roman side some of the details we already knew. It also shows that the events of Jesus' life had a significant enough impact around the Mediterranean to gain the attention (and disdain) of an elite Roman intellectual on the other side of the Empire. That a wandering Jewish peasant-teacher from Palestine rated a mention at all in Tacitus' *Annals of Imperial Rome* is surprising.

Lastly, another small piece of information deriving from the second century comes from a Jewish religious document called the **Talmud**. Although Jesus himself had been a popular Jewish teacher a century or so before, as time passed a number of very unflattering opinions were being formed about him:

> Jesus of Nazareth was hung up on the day of preparation for the Passover... because he practiced sorcery and he led Israel astray.
>
> *Baraitha Sanhedrin 43a*

It is difficult to know exactly what to make of this statement, since it is clearly a piece of official anti-Christian propaganda from a century or more after Jesus. Nevertheless, it does confirm that Jewish people of the second century thought Jesus to have been a real figure who had had a dramatic effect on many of their Palestinian Jewish forebears ('he lead Israel astray'). It also provides historians with another piece of corroborating evidence to support the wide-ranging claim that Jesus had performed unusual (miraculous?) feats. For it is curious that the statement makes no attempt to deny the rumoured exploits of Jesus. Instead, conceding that Jesus had inexplicable abilities, the document tries to explain them away as 'sorcery', something Jewish people were forbidden to be involved with.

If we piece together all the information contained in the above references it is fascinating that just about the whole story of Jesus can be uncovered, without even opening a Bible. We learn:

- when he lived
- where he lived
- that he was an influential teacher
- that he engaged in activities thought to be supernatural
- that he was executed; when and by whom
- that he had a brother called James who was also executed
- that people claimed to have seen him raised from the dead
- that he was widely known by the prestigious title 'the Christ'

This is a lot of material to glean from documents composed by people who were anything but supporters of the Christian faith.

None of these texts actually 'proves' Christianity. Statements made by non-Christians are no more trustworthy than those by Christians. From the historian's point of view, we must look at non-Christian accounts with the same healthy suspicion we apply to biblical documents. Nevertheless, the interesting thing is that whatever the sources, biases and (mis)information lying behind each of these documents, taken as a whole, they substantially corroborate the picture of Jesus presented in the earliest Christian literature. This is rather good news for anyone interested in enquiring into the Bible's version of the events surrounding Jesus' life. Indeed, one of Australia's most eminent ancient historians, Emeritus Professor E. A. Judge of Macquarie University, Sydney, has commented:

> An ancient historian has no problem seeing the phenomenon of Jesus as an historical one. His many surprising aspects only help anchor him in history. Myth or legend would have created a more predictable figure. The writings that sprang up about Jesus also reveal to us a movement of thought and an experience of life so unusual that something much more substantial than the imagination is needed to explain it.
>
> Quoted in P. Barnett, *The Truth about Jesus*, Aquila, Sydney, 1994

2. The Historical Reliability of the New Testament Documents

The 27 books of the New Testament were written between 40 and 100 AD. Few serious historians doubt this, nor is there much argument that what we read in our modern New Testaments is the same as what was originally written (except for some very minor variations). There are several reasons for this confidence.

A. The sheer number of early manuscripts

Although there are no copies of the original manuscripts in existence, we now have more than 24,000 early manuscript copies or portions of the New Testament. Around 5,300 of these are in Greek, and the remainder are early translations into other languages (such as Latin). By analysing this vast amount of manuscript evidence, it is possible to establish with a great deal of certainty a version of the text very close to the original.

B. The closeness in time to the original

Not only do we have a great many manuscripts, but a number of them are quite close in time to the original. The earliest manuscript portions date from 125 AD (although the recently discovered 'Jesus papyri' may date from around 70 AD); existing copies which contain much or all of the New Testament date from around 200 AD.

If this gap sounds like quite a period of time, it is worth making a comparison with other ancient documents, such as Homer's *Iliad*, or the works of Plato, Caesar or Sophocles. These ancient works, the authenticity of which no modern scholar would question, do not even come close to the New Testament in either the number of manuscripts or closeness in time to the original—as the following graph shows.

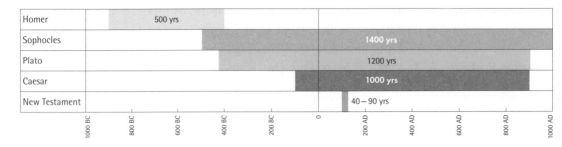

	● Homer	● Sophocles	● Plato	● Caesar	● New Testament
Number of copies found	643 copies	193 copies	7 copies	10 copies	24,000 copies
Time between writing and earliest surviving manuscripts	500 years later	1400 years later	1200 years later	1000 years later	40–90 years later

Sir Frederick Kenyon, former director and principal librarian of the British Museum puts it like this:

> The interval then between the dates of original composition and the earliest extant evidence becomes so small as to be in fact negligible, and the last foundation for any doubt that the Scriptures have come down to us substantially as they were written has now been removed. Both the authenticity and general integrity of the books of the New Testament may be regarded as finally established.
>
> F. Kenyon, *The Bible and Archaeology,* Harper and Row, New York, 1940, p. 288

3. Can we Trust the Gospels?

It is one thing to establish that the Gospels have come down to us as they were written, but can we trust that what they record is true? Is it possible that they are fictional, or partly fictional? Just how much can we trust the material in Jesus' biographies? The following short article by John Chapman addresses these questions.

Do you believe everything you read?

We are a strange mixture of gullibility and scepticism. If I say to you, "Do you believe everything you read in the newspaper?", you would probably say, "No". And I would agree. However, the fact is that we usually *do* believe it for no other reason than that it is printed in the paper! We may be more discriminating when it comes to television advertising. We know when the salesman says, "I wouldn't do this commercial if it were not true", that there's a better than even chance he is lying. However, when the newsreader appears on the box, meticulously groomed, dispensing information probably of unknown origin, but in such a cultured authoritative voice, then we will probably think what *he* says is true.

What makes an historical record accurate anyway? I would want to ask these questions: Was the writer an eyewitness to the event? If not, from where did he get his information? Do we have any verifying histories available from other authors? Were they published in the lifetime of eyewitnesses? How soon after the event were they written? Have they been transmitted accurately? Does the historian have an 'axe to grind' or some biased motive? Do his other utterances ring true?

When I submit the Gospels—Matthew, Mark, Luke and John—to these tests, I am satisfied that they do give us a reliable history of Jesus.

Were the Gospel writers eyewitnesses?

The apostles were with Jesus during his entire ministry. Matthew and John's Gospels are eyewitness accounts. There is an old but unproven tradition that Mark's Gospel is really the apostle Peter's account, recorded for him by Mark; Luke tells us that he himself is not an eyewitness but he also tells from where he got his information.

It is clear to any reader of the four Gospels that Matthew, Mark and Luke bear a strong similarity, although each has his distinctive style and aim. It still remains a matter of debate amongst New Testament scholars as to whether they copied from each other or whether they had access to some earlier documents which are now lost.

The Gospel of John, on the other hand, is quite independent. Apart from the death and resurrection of Jesus, he hardly duplicates any of the stories in the other Gospels. It seems as if he did not have access to the other Gospels at the time he wrote his. This means that we have at least two completely independent histories, which makes very valuable evidence. Often a document from antiquity stands alone with no other against which to check it. A good exercise would be to read Luke's Gospel and then John's. Then ask yourself, "Is the Jesus as portrayed in one, the same as in the other?" I am convinced he is, and it has given me much confidence in the Gospels as accurate, first hand, eyewitness accounts.

As you read through Matthew and John you will see the eyewitness touches about them. Matthew 28:17 is a good example. "When they saw him, they worshipped him; but some doubted". The piece of information "but some doubted" is an interesting sidelight. It doesn't do anything for the story or for the 'cause'. If anything it weakens the case for the resurrection. So why does Matthew insert it? Because he remembered it like that! Notice the eyewitness touch in John 6:10. It is the description of the feeding of the five thousand. "There was plenty of grass in that place, and the men sat down, about five thousand of them." No doubt you would remember the lush green of a pleasant spring picnic and even comment on it, but would you bother to say so if you hadn't been there?

Some years ago, a well known author and television script writer, Tony Morphett, became a Christian. Before that, by his own choice, he had been an atheist. A set of circumstances occurred which resulted in his reading the New Testament. He said that he was impressed with the Gospels: "I had spent all my working life writing scripts which were either documentary or fiction. When I came to the Gospels, I recognised that they were not fiction. They were documentary."

Paul Barnett, former Lecturer in New Testament History at Macquarie University and the University of Sydney, states: "While the Gospels have many distinctive features, they are in broad terms recognisable examples of history writers of their period. It is unhelpful and untrue to regard them merely as religious or theological works. They are also unmistakably historical in character. As historical sources of this period, they are just as valuable to the general historian as Josephus. Except, unlike Josephus, they are focused on one person and for a brief period."

Luke, on the other hand, tells us that he is not an eyewitness. The introduction to his Gospel shows historical method:

> Since many have attempted to put together an account of the things that have been fulfilled among us (just as these things were passed on to us by those who from the beginning were eyewitnesses and guardians of the message), so it seemed good to me as well, having checked everything very carefully from the start, to write something orderly for you, Your Excellency, Theophilus. My aim is that you may know the reliability of the reports you have hear. *(Luke 1:1-4)*

It is an interesting introduction written to his patron, Theophilus, of whom we know nothing. But its value lies in several areas. We know that at the time of writing this Gospel, there were many accounts of the sayings and actions of Jesus available. These accounts claimed to have been handed down from eyewitnesses. Luke is anxious that his patron should know "the certainty" about what he had heard. He wants him to be sure, so the most practical way to do that is to go back to square one himself. He has gone back to "eyewitnesses" so that "from the beginning" he might record an "orderly account".

That is the writer's stated aim. His historical method is sound and tells us the purpose of his book.

You may be interested to know that some of those other accounts have survived. The early church rejected them as accurate accounts either because they could not establish who the authors were or because they were proven to be forgeries.

But weren't they all biased?

It has often been said to me that the Gospel writers were all convinced Christians and so they must be biased in their approach. This is partly true. They were thoroughly convinced that Jesus is the unique Son of God. However, the prior question is: What caused them to be convinced? John tells us that he has become convinced about Jesus and he has recorded the reasons so that we can be convinced (John 20:31).

The Gospel writers, unlike many editorial writers, present their case and their personal interest and conviction right from the start and invite us to examine their conclusions. Sometimes they record incidents from the life of Jesus, sometimes they write editorial comments. It is easy to spot the difference. They make no effort to hide it. Most people don't go to the trouble to write a book unless they are really interested in the subject, and interest in the subject leads to greater attention to detail.

One of the characteristics which the Gospel writers claim for Jesus is that he was a person who told the truth and encouraged others to do so. Jesus claimed to be the embodiment of truth. He taught his disciples to love truth and to prize it highly. To be a disciple of Jesus means to do as Jesus did. Their interest in Jesus was likely to cause them to take greater care to check the facts than to make them up.

There is no doubt that they were convinced and completely absorbed by their subject. This is not the same as saying they must have been exaggerating because they were so convinced. If that were the case, it would mean we would never be able to get accurate information except from disinterested people. And disinterested people can often give us inaccurate accounts due to their lack of interest which causes them not to take care.

* Note on Josephus: Because of its obvious importance for our historical knowledge of Jesus, this passage is the subject of wide scholarly discussion. If you're keen to pursue further the content and significance of this quotation, and you have access to a major library, read C. A. Evans, *Noncanonical Writings and New Testament Interpretation,* Hendrickson Publishers, Massachusetts, 1992, pp. 86-96. The real glutton for punishment can read G. H. Twelftree, 'Jesus in Jewish Traditions', in *Gospel Perspectives: Studies of History and Tradition in the Four Gospels (Vol. 5),* JSOT Press, Manchester, 1981, pp. 289-341.

For further reading:
Paul Barnett, *The Truth about Jesus* (Aquila Press, 1994)
Paul Barnett, *Is the New Testament History?* (Paternoster, 1998)
Craig Blomberg, *The historical reliability of the Gospels* (IVP, 1987)

Pages 33-37 of this Extra Information compiled by Tony Payne. Material by John Chapman taken from A Fresh Start (Matthias Media, 1997).

SESSION

2

IN THE PRESENCE
OF GREATNESS

1. The Story So Far

Christianity at its heart is not about rules or rituals but about a person, Jesus Christ —a person we can get to know by reading the Gospel of Luke.

2. A Great Title

"Christ" (read Luke 2:1-12). The one invested with God's authority.

3. Great Actions

- Authority as God's spokesperson (read Luke 4:14-22)
- Authority to heal people (read Luke 4:38-40)
- Authority to hand out God's forgiveness (read Luke 5:17-26)
- Authority to lead people (read Luke 5:27-28)

4. Recognizing Greatness

"Who do you say I am?" (read Luke 9:18-22).

5. The Big Idea

As the Christ, Jesus possessed the authority of God himself. It is an authority he calls on people to recognize.

6. At Home

For next week please read Luke 10-19 (or 15:1-19:10 if you are short of time). Look out for hints of what Jesus thought was his central mission. Note down anything you don't understand, or would like to discuss. We'll have a time for discussion next week.

The Gospel of Luke, Chapters 1-9

Depending on your group's confidence with each other, begin a discussion about what they feel makes a good leader—a political leader, sporting leader or whatever. Allow just 2-3 minutes for this then explain that today's/tonight's session touches on Jesus' leadership credentials.

Alternatively, just begin as below...

1. The Story So Far

- Welcome to Session Two. I hope you found the at-home reading manageable and interesting and that you have come today/tonight with your questions.
- There was really only one big idea in last week's Session...

Christianity at its heart is not about rules or rituals but about a person, Jesus Christ—a person we can get to know by reading the Gospel of Luke.

- You might also remember from last week the working definition of Christianity: "Responding appropriately to Jesus Christ".
- Today/tonight we're going to build on that starting point by asking: Who did Jesus claim to be?

2. A Great Title

- Jesus is often portrayed in images of weakness and humility. Paintings, stained glass windows and some of the old Hollywood Jesus movies often present Jesus as a harmless, passive fellow who only ever spoke about being nice to people. But such images hardly square with the portrait of Jesus found in the opening chapters of Luke's Gospel.
- To begin with Luke refers to Jesus by a very prestigious title...

"Christ" (read Luke 2:1-12). The one invested with God's authority.

- The word 'Christ' is often used as a kind of surname for Jesus, as if his parents were Mary and Joseph Christ and he just inherited the name.
- But, of course, 'Christ' is a title. And it's a title with a big history.
- The word literally means 'anointed one' and is a reference to God's anointing someone with power.
- For instance, throughout the 'Old Testament'—the Jewish scriptures written centuries before Christ—God's appointed kings were called 'anointed ones'. In fact, the coronation ceremony of ancient Israelite kings involved a priest pouring a large jar of (fine Middle Eastern) olive oil over the new king. This 'anointing' symbolized the outpouring of God's authority upon this individual.
- This important idea gave rise to prophecies and expectations that one day the truly Anointed One would come and rule with God's authority. This person, the 'Christ', would be anointed not symbolically with olive oil but in reality with a full measure of God's own Spirit, and as such he would speak and act on God's behalf. If you're

interested in reading some of those prophecies from the Old Testament, the Extra Information for today's session contains a brief account.

- The important thing for us to note is that when Jesus is announced in Luke 2:11 as the 'Christ', it was not simply a casual explanation of his full name but a clarification of his status as the promised king, the one invested with God's authority to speak and act.
- Are there any questions about the title 'Christ' and what it means?
- Exactly how Jesus went on to reveal his status as the 'Christ' is the concern of the rest of Luke's Gospel. We're now going to look at a few of the more important paragraphs in this respect.

3. Great Actions

Jesus' authority as the Christ is described in many different ways throughout Luke 1-9.

Authority as God's spokesperson
(read Luke 4:14–22)

- The passage Jesus read in the synagogue (a Jewish 'church') was written hundreds of years before he was even born. Yet Jesus claims this passage was all about him. As verse 21 says, "Today this Scripture is fulfilled in your hearing."
- The claim is even more staggering when we note what the Old Testament prophecy is saying about Jesus. It says that Jesus has been 'anointed' (as the Christ) with God's Spirit in order to make statements on God's behalf. In other words, Jesus

proclaims God's words. To hear Jesus is to hear the voice of God.

- There are so many voices in our world competing for our attention: politicians try to tell us how to think and vote; advertisers tell us what to buy; therapists and talk show hosts endeavour to tell us what's important in life; and so on. Throughout the story of Luke, we'll often hear of people being amazed at Jesus' words. This is because as the Christ—the one who speaks on God's behalf—Jesus is a clear and healthy voice amidst all the noise of the others'.

Authority to heal people
(read Luke 4:38–40)

- It might be tempting for some of us to dismiss Jesus' miracles of healings as the talk of an ancient writer who didn't know anything about medical science. But ancient Jews did know about natural medicine, and Luke himself was a medical doctor. Nevertheless, the reports of Jesus' power to heal are so widespread, it is difficult to quickly dismiss their historical reality. One anti-Christian document from the period (written by Jewish leaders some time after Jesus) even concedes Jesus' ability to engage in miracles.
- It's important, though, not to see Jesus' healings merely as 'party-tricks' or proofs of his power. They are actually signs of God's intention one day to heal all the brokenness of our world. What Jesus did in history was a kind of pledge of the reality that will exist in God's eternal kingdom.

Authority to hand out God's forgiveness (read Luke 5:17-26)

- The amazing thing about this episode in Jesus' life is not the adventurous way these friends got Jesus' attention. It's not even that Jesus was able to heal a disabled man. The truly incredible thing is that Jesus claimed to be able to forgive people for the wrongs they have committed against God and fellow humanity.

- Imagine I stole your purse/wallet and later met someone (other than you) who said they forgave me for stealing your wallet. You would feel upset and cheated, wouldn't you? No one can hand out your forgiveness but you, surely! But here is Jesus saying that he can hand out God's forgiveness. As controversial as it was to the religious leaders of the day (in v.21) these actions point again to Jesus' status as the Christ, the bringer of God's forgiveness.

- Life can sometimes be very unforgiving. Sometimes people hold grudges to their deathbed. Sometimes a simple mistake at work can hinder the progress of a career. Sometimes an angry word can divide friends for years. But with God, there is forgiveness for all who want it. And Jesus is the one with the authority to hand it out.

Authority to lead people (read Luke 5:27-28)

- This is perhaps the most interesting aspect of Jesus' authority as the Christ. He regularly asks men and women to give him their allegiance, to follow him as their leader. And he expects them to obey.

- But we shouldn't view this negatively. Following Jesus was not a hindrance to life, something to feel nervous or depressed about. It is fascinating to note in verse 29 that Levi's first act as a follower of Jesus is to throw a party in honour of Jesus. Following Jesus is something worth celebrating and inviting your friends along to.

4. Recognizing Greatness

"Who do you say I am?"
(read Luke 9:18-22)

- This passage is the climax so far in Luke's biography. Jesus asks a very confronting question of his disciples: "Who do you say I am?" After all they had seen over the last year or so—Jesus' authority to speak for God, to heal diseases, to forgive people's past, and to lead people—this is a question they would have thought very seriously about.

- Peter answers with great simplicity, and no doubt with a high degree of reverence: "You are the Christ of God." Peter and the disciples finally realise what we've known from chapter two— that Jesus is God's anointed leader.

Provide time for questions now. After questions, you may like to show a section of the Jesus video—from the calming of the storm to Peter's confession of Jesus as the Messiah.

Wrap up by reading the Big Idea.

5. The Big Idea

As the Christ, Jesus possessed the authority of God himself. It is an authority he calls on people to recognize.

- Jesus asked those around him: "Who do you say I am?" It's a question Luke obviously wants his readers to ask themselves. So as we go today/tonight, try and spend some time reflecting upon who you think Jesus is.

At Home

For next week please read Luke 10–19 (or 15:1–19:10 if you are short of time). Look out for hints of what Jesus thought was his central mission. Note down anything you don't understand, or would like to discuss. We'll have a time for discussion next week.

- Thank you very much for coming; please stay for more food and drink, or feel free to go when you need to.

EXTRA INFORMATION
FOR SESSION TWO

Old Testament Prophecies
Concerning the Coming King/Christ

The 'anointing' ceremony of King David

In about 1000 BC a young man called David son of Jesse (of 'David and Goliath' fame) was selected to be the first in a long line of dynastic kings to rule ancient Israel. The ceremony by which he is made king establishes the importance of 'anointing' for the future hope concerning the 'Anointed One', or the Christ.

> The LORD said to Samuel, "How long will you grieve over Saul, since I have rejected him from being king over Israel? Fill your horn with oil, and go. I will send you to Jesse the Bethlehemite, for I have provided for myself a king among his sons." And Samuel said, "How can I go? If Saul hears it, he will kill me." And the LORD said, "Take a heifer with you and say, 'I have come to sacrifice to the LORD.' And invite Jesse to the sacrifice, and I will show you what you shall do. And you shall anoint for me him whom I declare to you." Samuel did what the LORD commanded and came to Bethlehem. The elders of the city came to meet him trembling and said, "Do you come peaceably?" And he said, "Peaceably; I have come to sacrifice to the LORD. Consecrate yourselves, and come with me to the sacrifice." And he consecrated Jesse and his sons and invited them to the sacrifice.
>
> When they came, he looked on Eliab and thought, "Surely the LORD's anointed is before him." But the LORD said to Samuel, "Do not look on his appearance or on the height of his stature, because I have rejected him. For the LORD sees not as man sees: man looks on the outward appearance, but the LORD looks on the heart." Then Jesse called Abinadab and made him pass before Samuel. And he said, "Neither has the LORD chosen this one." Then Jesse made Shammah pass by. And he said, "Neither has the LORD chosen this one." And Jesse made seven of his sons pass before Samuel. And Samuel said to Jesse, "The LORD has not chosen these." Then Samuel said to Jesse, "Are all your sons here?" And he said, "There remains yet the youngest, but behold, he is keeping the sheep." And Samuel said to Jesse, "Send and get him, for we will not sit down till he comes here." And he sent and brought him in. Now he was ruddy and had beautiful eyes and was handsome. And the LORD said, "Arise, anoint him, for this is he." Then Samuel took the horn of oil and anointed him in the midst of his brothers. And the Spirit of the LORD rushed upon David from that day forward. And Samuel rose up and went to Ramah. *(1 Samuel 16:1-13)*

Each king of Israel from this time on was occasionally known as an 'anointed one' (a messiah or christ). But it was not until much later (about 200 BC) that Jewish people were crying out for the *anointed one*, the Christ of God. The language of this hope (Christ) derived from the coronation ceremony described above, but the real substance of the hope came directly from a number of prophecies contained in the pages of the Old Testament which predicted the arrival of a descendant of King David who would speak and act on behalf of the Almighty and rule the nations for ever. Below is a brief outline of some of the elements of these promises.

The Promise of an Eternal King

Despite the length and greatness of King David's reign, the prophet Nathan promised David on God's behalf that one of his descendants would become even greater. According to the prophecy, this heir would rule for all of history.

> But that same night the word of the LORD came to Nathan, "Go and tell my servant David, 'Thus says the LORD...When your days are fulfilled and you lie down with your fathers, I will raise up your offspring after you, who shall come from your body, and I will establish his kingdom. He shall build a house for my name, and I will establish the throne of his kingdom forever. I will be to him a father, and he shall be to me a son...And your house and your kingdom shall be made sure forever before me. Your throne shall be established forever.'" In accordance with all these words, and in accordance with all this vision, Nathan spoke to David. *(2 Samuel 7:4-17)*

In a matter of generations after King David, Israel and its kings sank into religious, political and military turmoil. To cut a long story short, by 587 BC the Jewish people had been reduced to prisoners in their own land. Foreign armies invaded and virtually destroyed them. The old promise of a descendant of King David who would rule forever seemed like a dim and ridiculous hope.

There were some, however, who during the final years of Israel's royal history did remember the promise Nathan relayed to King David. These people were the 'prophets' and they preached and wrote enthusiastically during a time of great pessimism about God's intention one day to send that leader of their dreams. Their writings, contained now in the Old Testament part of the Bible, provide the clearest predictions about the 'Anointed One', the descendant of David who would reign eternally.

Here are four of the most significant prophecies concerning the eternal king, all of which were written hundreds of years before the birth of Jesus.

Ezekiel 37:22-25 (600BC)

> "And one king shall be king over them all, and they shall be no longer two nations, and no longer divided into two kingdoms. They shall not defile themselves anymore with their idols and their detestable things, or with any of their transgressions. But I

will save them from all the backslidings in which they have sinned, and will cleanse them; and they shall be my people, and I will be their God.

"My servant David shall be king over them, and they shall all have one shepherd. They shall walk in my rules and be careful to obey my statutes. They shall dwell in the land that I gave to my servant Jacob, where your fathers lived. They and their children and their children's children shall dwell there forever, and David my servant shall be their prince forever."

Calling the future king "David" is a deliberate reflection on the promise quoted earlier that one of King David's son's will arise. Like that original promise, this prophecy also insists the king will rule forever. It is difficult to know how the Jews of this period would have understood this promise, since they, like us, knew that people do not live forever.

The Gospels of Luke and Matthew both begin with Jesus' genealogical records, establishing him as a direct descendant of King David, and they both end (as do all the Gospels) with the account of Jesus' resurrection. It is his resurrection, according to Jesus himself, that ensures his status as the king who rules forever.

The other interesting thing about this prophecy is that the arrival of the king will mark a time of forgiveness for past wrongs. As the story of Jesus unfolds, precisely this theme is highlighted again and again.

Micah 5:2 (700BC)

A brief, though important, prophecy concerns the whereabouts of the coming ruler. In his prediction about what God would do for his people, Micah writes:

But you, O Bethlehem Ephrathah, who are too little to be among the clans of Judah, from you shall come forth for me one who is to be ruler in Israel, whose origin is from of old, from ancient days.

Bethlehem is a small town in the South of Palestine, 10 kilometres from the city of Jerusalem. Though small and apparently insignificant, it did have at least one claim to fame. It was the birthplace and family home town of the great King David 500 years before. According to this prophecy, it would have an even greater claim to fame in the future. It would be the place from which the "ruler over Israel" (in other words, the promised anointed king) would come. Jesus, as we know from Luke (and elsewhere), was in fact born in the city of David, Bethlehem.

Isaiah 9:1–7 (700BC)

But there will be no gloom for her who was in anguish. In the former time he brought into contempt the land of Zebulun and the land of Naphtali, but in the latter time he has made glorious the way of the sea, the land beyond the Jordan, Galilee of the nations. The people who walked in darkness have seen a great light; those who dwelt in a land of deep darkness, on them has light shined. You have multiplied the nation; you have increased its joy; they rejoice before you as with joy at the harvest, as they are glad when they divide the spoil...For to us a child is born, to us a son is given; and the government shall be upon his shoulder, and his name shall be called Wonderful Counselor, Mighty God, Everlasting Father, Prince of Peace. Of the increase of his government and of peace there will be no end, on the throne of David and over his kingdom, to establish it and to uphold it with justice and with righteousness from this time forth and forevermore. The zeal of the LORD of hosts will do this.

Here God promises that the Northern region of Palestine, Galilee, which was first to be decimated and overrun by 'Gentiles' (700 BC), will become the very district from which a great 'light' will appear. This will be the cause of great 'rejoicing' since the light turns out to be none other than the promised descendant of King David who would emerge from Galilee and rule forever.

On the face of it, this appears to contradict the prophecy of Micah that the promised 'ruler' would come from Bethlehem in the South of the country. For years, anyone who put these two texts side by side must have wondered how the anointed descendant of King David could come from both the Southern town of Bethlehem and the Northern district of Galilee, over a hundred kilometres away.

Though Jesus was born in the South (Bethlehem) of Palestine, this was only because of an unexpected Imperial requirement in that precise year that all Jews return to the town of their ancestors so that a documented census could take place throughout the land. Jesus' real home town—where he spent his entire childhood, right up to the time of his inaugural sermon—was, in fact, Nazareth, a town in the Northern district of Galilee. When the 'light' of Jesus' ministry appeared to the public eye, it was out of Galilee that it first shone.

Isaiah 11:1-10 (700 BC)

Here the coming king is described as a 'shoot' from the 'stump of Jesse'. Jesse was King David's father. By the time Isaiah wrote these words this family dynasty was in tatters and on the verge of total destruction, which is why it is described as a 'stump' instead of a whole tree. Nevertheless, the prophecy is clear: from this family line a 'branch' will grow.

There shall come forth a shoot from the stump of Jesse, and a branch from his roots shall bear fruit. And the Spirit of the LORD shall rest upon him, the Spirit of wisdom and understanding, the Spirit of counsel and might, the Spirit of knowledge and the fear of the LORD. And his delight shall be in the fear of the LORD. He shall not judge by what his eyes see, or decide disputes by what his ears hear, but with righteousness he shall judge the poor, and decide with equity for the meek of the earth; and he shall strike the earth with the rod of his mouth, and with the breath of his lips he shall kill the wicked. Righteousness shall be the belt of his waist, and faithfulness the belt of his loins. The wolf shall dwell with the lamb, and the leopard shall lie down with the young goat, and the calf and the lion and the fattened calf together; and a little child shall lead them. The cow and the bear shall graze; their young shall lie down together; and the lion shall eat straw like the ox. The nursing child shall play over the hole of the cobra, and the weaned child shall put his hand on the adder's den. They shall not hurt or destroy in all my holy mountain; for the earth shall be full of the knowledge of the LORD as the waters cover the sea. In that day the root of Jesse, who shall stand as a signal for the peoples—of him shall the nations inquire, and his resting place shall be glorious.

There are several important aspects of this prophecy. First, this descendant of David is described as ruling with his 'mouth', that is, by the mere force of his words. This must have sounded unusual to its first hearers since they must certainly have felt that what they needed was not a 'talker' but 'warrior'. Jesus worked hard at dispelling the view that his was going to be a reign of warfare. Instead, he was indeed a great teacher. By his words he ruled.

Furthermore, it is odd that this coming king would be rallied to not only by Israel but also by all the nations. This idea was quite contrary to the political mood of both Isaiah's time and Jesus' time. The 'nations' were regarded as the enemies of God and Israel. Nevertheless, the prophecy is adamant that "The Root of Jesse will stand as a banner for the peoples; the nations will rally to him". In other words, this was a king for the world not just the Jews. This ends up being one of the very striking features of Jesus' ministry. He had an unusual openness to non-Jews whenever he met them. And in his final words to his colleagues he insisted that the news of his reign as the Christ must be "announced to all nations, beginning from Jerusalem" (Luke 24:47).

Isaiah 52:13 – 53:12 (700 BC)

The final and most striking prophecy I will quote (though there are many others) comes again from the prophet Isaiah. Here Isaiah speaks of the appearance of a mysterious figure known as the 'Servant'. There are no names or dates provided, but he is described as a "tender shoot" who "grew up out of the dry ground". This is clearly a reference back to the prophecy just quoted about the 'shoot' that grew up out of the 'stump of Jesse'. In other words, both prophecies are a reference to the promised descendant of King David. But there is an extraordinary difference between this and all the other prophecies about the future anointed king. Whereas most of the prophecies describe this figure as a powerful and majestic monarch, someone who rules the nations forever merely by the words of his mouth, the promise of Isaiah 52–53 describes him as a suffering and dying 'servant'. The passage is long but it is remarkable when you keep in mind that we know this was written hundreds of years before the birth of Jesus of Nazareth.

Behold, my servant shall act wisely; he shall be high and lifted up, and shall be exalted. As many were astonished at you—his appearance was so marred, beyond human semblance, and his form beyond that of the children of mankind—so shall he sprinkle many nations; kings shall shut their mouths because of him; for that which has not been told them they see, and that which they have not heard they understand.

Who has believed what they heard from us? And to whom has the arm of the LORD been revealed? For he grew up before him like a young plant, and like a root out of dry ground; he had no form or majesty that we should look at him, and no beauty that we should desire him. He was despised and rejected by men; a man of sorrows, and acquainted with grief; and as one from whom men hide their faces he was despised, and we esteemed him not. Surely he has borne our griefs and carried our sorrows; yet we esteemed him stricken, smitten by God, and afflicted. But he was wounded for our transgressions; he was crushed for our iniquities; upon him was the chastisement that brought us peace, and with his stripes we are healed.

All we like sheep have gone astray; we have turned every one to his own way; and the LORD has laid on him the iniquity of us all. He was oppressed, and he was afflicted, yet he opened not his mouth; like a lamb that is led to the slaughter, and like a sheep that before its shearers is silent, so he opened not his mouth. By oppression and judgment he was taken away; and as for his generation, who considered that he was cut off out of the land of the living, stricken for the transgression of my people? And they made his grave with the wicked and with a rich man in his death, although he had done no violence, and there was no deceit in his mouth. Yet it was the will of the LORD to crush him; he has put him to grief; when his soul makes an offering for sin, he shall see his offspring; he shall prolong his days; the will of the LORD shall prosper in his hand. Out of the anguish of his soul he shall see and be satisfied; by his knowledge shall the righteous one, my servant, make many to be accounted righteous, and he shall bear their iniquities. Therefore I will divide him a portion with the many, and he shall divide the spoil with the strong, because he poured out his soul to death and was numbered with the transgressors; yet he bore the sin of many, and makes intercession for the transgressors.

I've known about this prophecy for over a decade but I am still amazed by its message. This 'Servant' of God would not attain 'majesty' but instead be 'pierced' and 'wounded'. He would die a horrible death—"cut off from the land of the living"—for the sake of others. He was punished for the sins of others so they could be forgiven. Eventually, however, this Servant would again "prolong his days" and "see the light of life". In other words, he would be raised from death. This story of tragedy to triumph would, according to the introduction to the prophecy, touch the world; he would "sprinkle many nations".

For a text composed 700 years before Christ this is not a bad summary of the story of Jesus Christ, the promised descendant of David who since his life, death and resurrection has, indeed, 'sprinkled' many nations.

Miracles

Miracles are an integral part of the story of Jesus. Taking just the first nine chapters of Luke (which we've been reading), we are told not only about the extraordinary circumstances of his birth, but the numerous exorcisms that he performs, the dramatic healings of lepers and paralytics, and even the raising of two dead children back to life. Add to this the stilling of the storm (in chapter 8) and the feeding of the five thousand (in chapter 9), and you have a picture of someone with extraordinary power.

There is little doubt, historically speaking, that Jesus was famous as a miracle worker. The many stories of his miracles are spread throughout the four Gospels, and even Josephus, the Jewish historian, records that Jesus was known for his 'surprising feats'.

We will come back to consider why Jesus' miracles are important, and what they mean, but first we need to deal with a more basic issue. Can we, as modern people, believe that these miracles really happened? Can we accept that the laws of nature were broken or suspended so that Jesus could walk on water, or feed thousands of people with a single cut lunch? These stories seem so strange to us, so outside our experience, that we almost instinctively doubt their credibility.

Can we believe in miracles? And if we can't, can we believe in Jesus?

Before we answer these questions, there is a more basic problem to solve.

1. What are 'miracles'?

The first step towards understanding the miracles of Jesus (and the Bible generally) is to understand what Luke and the other Bible writers thought a 'miracle' was. This is because they thought about the whole subject very differently from most 20th century people.

How modern people regard miracles

For us, a 'miracle' is where the normal laws of nature are supposedly suspended or broken, indicating that some 'god' or supernatural force has been active. Someone might be 'miraculously' healed of cancer, for instance, and since there is no other explanation available, we shake our heads and say "Well, maybe there is a God after all".

This way of viewing miracles stems from how 20th century Western people think about the world in general. Most of us assume that the world is like a giant complex machine or organism, with millions of interlocking parts. Science has discovered how many of these parts work, and has formulated laws and principles by which we can predict how 'the machine' will operate. According to this way of thinking, the world runs along under its own steam. If there is a 'God', then he might have been responsible for designing the world, and even setting it running, but he isn't involved in its day-to-day operations. In fact, the only way you know he exists is when he puts his fingers into the machine and dabbles with it, producing what we call a 'miracle'.

How the Bible regards miracles

In many respects, people in biblical times thought very differently from us, not only about miracles, but about the world in general. But this is not to say that they thought completely differently.

They knew, for example, that the world was a regular and orderly place. Like us, they noticed the patterns of nature—day and night, the seasons, and the rain. They knew that if you dropped something, it fell, and that if you stood on water, you would sink. They understood that the world operated according to certain patterns and you could make the most of these in order to live successfully—for example, if you planted your seed at the right time of year, in the right kind of soil, under the right weather conditions, you could be fairly certain of getting a good crop.

However, unlike us, they regarded all this is as being the work of God. They saw the world not as an independently operating machine, but as something that God had made and continued to sustain and uphold. It was God who caused the sun to rise, the rain to fall and the seasons to come and go. They knew God to be the sovereign ruler of all things, who kept everything going in his great power and wisdom. And precisely because he was in charge of everything, God could change his normal way of doing things and act in an amazing or unusual way, if it suited him.

This way of thinking about the world is often called 'theism'. According to biblical theism, a miracle is not God sticking his finger into the works of the machine so as to prove his existence. It is simply God working outside his normal regular patterns.

This, then, was what the writers of the Bible (like Luke) thought a 'miracle' was— some work of God that was surprising or noteworthy or unusual, and which was performed for some important reason.

2. The modern objection to miracles

With this background in mind, it is not difficult to see that many of the objections that people have to the miracles of the Bible are either not very relevant or not very clever.

Some have argued, for example, that because 1st century people were primitive and did not understand science, they were prepared to believe anything. However, this is hardly reasonable. 1st century people, like us, knew that dead people stayed dead. That was their experience, as it is ours. That is why they mourned, as we do. They also knew that people who had been paralytics for 30 years didn't suddenly get up and start walking. And this is precisely why they called it a 'miracle' or a 'wonder' when Jesus raised the dead girl to life, or healed the paralytic. They believed that the God who ruled the world was well able to do such things, and regarded it as an amazing and exciting occurrence when he did so.

Another argument against miracles is that it is so unlikely that a genuine miracle would ever happen that we should dismiss all claims of miracles as being inherently unreliable. According to this argument, it is much more likely that the people involved were mistaken or deceived or were themselves deceivers—and so we should not trust their testimony. This approach has a number of problems, not the least of which is that it rules out testimony about all unusual or extraordinary events. Take for example the following occurrences:

- In Greenberry Hill, London, in 1641, three men were hanged for the murder of a local magistrate. By pure coincidence, their surnames were Green, Berry and Hill.
- In the mid-1700s, a Russian peasant named Feodor Vassileyev gave birth to 69 children. In 27 separate pregnancies, she had 16 pairs of twins, seven sets of triplets, and four sets of quadruplets.
- In 1664, 1785 and 1860, three separate passenger ferries sank while crossing the Menai straight off North Wales. Amazingly, each disaster occurred on December 5th. More bizarre than this, however, is that on all three occasions there was only one survivor, and in each case his name was Hugh Williams.

Each of these events is strange, unusual, and highly unlikely. Yet there is excellent historical evidence that they all, in fact, occurred. Extraordinary things do occur. That they don't occur very often is what makes them extraordinary!

To say, therefore, that the miracles attributed to Jesus could not have happened, simply because they are beyond our own normal experience, is to prejudge the question entirely. It is to make up our minds without looking at the evidence. It is like someone who lives in the tropics refusing to believe in the possibility of such a thing as ice, simply because they have never seen or touched it.

If theism is true, then the occurrence of miracles is quite reasonable. Miracles are simply the extraordinary (as opposed to the ordinary) workings of the God who made the world and continues to rule it. What is more, if Jesus is God's representative—if he speaks and acts with all the power and authority of God—then it would seem quite consistent for him to be able to perform what we could call 'miraculous' feats. If theism, and Christianity, is true, then the miracles recorded of Jesus are almost to be expected.

The first thing to work out, then, is whether theism (and Christianity) is true. And that is one of the purposes of the *Simply Christianity* course.

One final thing needs to be said about the miracles of Jesus.

3. The meaning of the miracles

We have already said that for Luke (and the other Bible writers) miracles were not some proof of God's existence. They already knew that God existed and was powerfully in control of the world. Miracles were simply God acting in a striking or amazing way to achieve a particular purpose. In other words, the important thing about the miracles of Jesus is not so much that they happened, *but what they signified or meant.*

We get an important clue to the meaning of Jesus' miracles from this episode in

Luke, chapter 7:

> The men came to Jesus and said, "John the Baptist sent us to you to ask, 'Are you
> the Coming One or should we wait for another?'". At that particular time, Jesus
> healed many people from illnesses and diseases and evil spirits, and he gave many
> blind people back their sight. He answered the men, "Go back and tell John what
> you see and hear: the blind see, the crippled walk, and the lepers are being
> cleansed; the deaf hear, the dead are being raised, and the poor are hearing the
> great news. And blessed is the one who does not stumble because of me."
>
> *(Luke 7:20-23)*

In response to John's enquiry about whether he really was 'the one', Jesus sends back
the report of all the miracles he has been doing (as well as his preaching of the good
news). Clearly, Jesus thinks this is all the answer John should need. And in light of the
Old Testament, it was. John, like Simeon and Anna (of Luke Chapter 2) and many of
the Israelites of his time, was looking forward to the Messiah, the One who would come
in God's name as God's ruler, to bring redemption and victory for Israel. The Old
Testament prophets had promised that this would happen in passages like this one:

> Say to those who have an anxious heart, "Be strong; fear not! Behold, your God will
> come with vengeance, with the recompense of God. He will come and save you."
> Then the eyes of the blind shall be opened, and the ears of the deaf unstopped;
> then shall the lame man leap like a deer, and the tongue of the mute sing for joy.
> For waters break forth in the wilderness, and streams in the desert. *(Isaiah 35:4-6)*

Or the passage from Isaiah that Jesus quoted in the synagogue in Nazareth:

> "The Spirit of the Lord is upon me, because he has anointed me to announce great
> news to the poor; he has sent me to proclaim release for prisoners, and sight once
> more for the blind, to send the oppressed away free; to proclaim the acceptable
> year of the Lord". *(Luke 4:18-19 quoting Isaiah 61:1-2)*

The miracles that Jesus performed were the signs of the Messiah. They were the
powerful indication that God had fulfilled his ancient promises, that the time had come,
and that 'the One' that Israel had waited so long for had arrived.

Extra Information on 'Miracles' compiled by Tony Payne.

For further reading:
Kirsten Birkett, *Unnatural Enemies: an introduction to Science and Christianity,*
(Matthias Media, 1997).

SESSION

3

SEARCH AND RESCUE

1. The Story So Far

Christianity is about responding appropriately to Jesus Christ.

As the 'Christ', Jesus possessed the authority of God himself.

2. Jesus: The Rescuer

Jesus was designated 'Saviour' (or 'Rescuer') because he would rescue or 'save' people (read Luke 2:11).

3. Jesus and Judgement

Examples include Luke 10:13-15; 11:31-32).
Read Luke 13:22-30.

4. Jesus and the Rescue of 'Sinners'

Read Luke 15.

- Who is the 'sinner' (look closely at 15:11-13)? What is his 'sin'?
- What is God like (look closely at 15:20-24)?

5. The Big Idea

Jesus was God's 'rescuer'. His aim was to find people who have distanced themselves from God and deserve his judgement, and convince them to return home and offer them a fresh start.

6. At Home

For next week please read Luke 20-23 and ask yourself: Why was it necessary for Jesus to die? Note down anything you don't understand, or would like to discuss. We'll have a time for discussion next week.

The Gospel of Luke, Chapters 10-19

1. The Story So Far

Christianity is about responding appropriately to Jesus Christ.

As the 'Christ', Jesus possessed the authority of God himself.

- Last week, then, our focus was Jesus' status or identity as the Christ. This week we're looking at his *mission*.

2. Jesus: The Rescuer

- We have already seen that Jesus was known by a prestigious title—the Christ. But at his birth he was given another title also.

Jesus was designated 'Saviour' (or 'Rescuer') because he would rescue or 'save' people (read Luke 2:11).

- But this theme is not only conveyed in the title, 'Saviour', it is implied in the very name 'Jesus' as well. Each of our names has some meaning: for instance, my name _____ means _____. (You can easily find baby name information on the internet.) The word 'Jesus' literally means 'God *saves or rescues*'. By title and by name, Jesus' mission concerned rescue.
- But, of course, this raises the questions: Whom was Jesus to save? And, from what was he to save them?
- The answer has to do with the Old Testament theme of God's judgement.

3. Jesus and Judgement (examples include Luke 10:13-15; 11:31-32)

- From your reading of Luke's Gospel you will have noticed that Jesus never shied away from addressing the theme of divine judgement (examples include: 10:13-15; 11:31-32). As unpopular as this theme has become in modern society it is an unavoidable aspect of Jesus' message.
- In fact, Jesus went so far as to say that, as the Christ, God had appointed him as the administrator of God's judgements. In Luke 13, someone asks him whether many will be saved from judgement. His response was intriguing.

Read Luke 13:22-30

- Clearly, the one who "ate and drank... and taught" in their streets is Jesus himself. But he is also described in this analogy as "the owner of the house", that is, the one with the authority to open or shut the door of God's kingdom on the people of the world.
- On the one hand, it's comforting to know that someone as humble, just and compassionate as Jesus is in charge of the judgement. But, on the other, it's unnerving to know that this same Jesus was the one who was so outraged by hypocrisy, greed and injustice in all its forms.
- This passage should begin to make us wonder whether we will be among those 'welcomed in' to God's kingdom, so to speak, or 'locked out'.

- The Extra Information for Session Three explores the theme of God's judgement. Feel free to read that and ask questions next week.
- There was something unique about Jesus' approach to the question of God's judgement. And because of it Jesus often clashed with the religious leaders of his day.

4. Jesus and the Rescue of 'Sinners'

- Jesus was famous for wining and dining with precisely the sorts of people one would normally have expected to deserve judgement, the so-called 'sinners'. In fact, in Luke 7:34 we learn that the religious leaders were beginning to slander Jesus calling him a "glutton and a drunkard, a friend of tax collectors and 'sinners'."
- So, on the one hand, Jesus insisted that God would one day judge men and women for every act of human evil and injustice. But, on the other hand, he displayed an unusual preference for being with and befriending those who had offended God the most.
- On one occasion Jesus stopped to explain this apparent contradiction. In doing so, he left us with a clear explanation of his mission as the saviour.

Read Luke 15

- According to the opening lines of this chapter, Jesus was again in trouble with the religious leaders for befriending "sinners and tax-collectors". The word

'sinner' was a common way of referring to someone considered to be under God's judgement. 'Tax collectors' were often dishonest businessmen and so were a particularly notable class of 'sinner'.
- The three stories Jesus tells are designed to explain why he befriends 'sinners'. The third story, the famous 'Prodigal Son', is particularly important. In it Jesus offers both his own definition of the 'sinner' and his own description of God.

Who is the 'sinner' (look closely at 15:11–13)? What is his 'sin'?

- The wayward younger son obviously represents the sinners Jesus has been befriending, just as the complaining elder son represents the religious leaders and the father represents God. As such, Jesus' description of the young son provides a glimpse into what Jesus thought made a person a 'sinner'.
- Our society often associates the word 'sin' with big, individual, immoral acts such as murder, theft, adultery, etc. On this definition many of us I assume could claim NOT to be sinners.
- But Jesus' understanding of sin is more subtle and more unsettling. The main offense of this young man was not that he ended up in 'wild living'. It was that he demanded his share of his father's resources and then decided to spend those resources on himself, at a great distance from the father. In other words, he wanted all that his father had to offer, but nothing to do with the father himself.
- On this definition of sin, how many of us can claim NOT to be 'sinners'? We, like the son in Jesus' story, keenly stake

our claim on God's resources of life, relationships, food, money and the environment, but at the same time keep our distance from God himself, either by decision or neglect. We rarely thank him, honour him, or even seek his advice on how his resources should be invested. We may not live 'wildly' but we do live 'separately' from the Father. This is at the heart of 'sin', according to Jesus.

- But Jesus not only has a striking definition of sin, he has a unique description of God. And it's this understanding of God's personality that drives Jesus' friendships with 'sinners'.

What is God like (look closely at 15:20–24)?

- Notice a few beautiful elements of father's reaction: first, in verse 20, the father sees the son while he was "still a long way off", implying he was on the lookout for the son; secondly, in the rest of verse 20, the father runs, embraces and kisses the son even before he has heard the son's apology; and thirdly, no sooner does the son offer his apology than the father, in verses 22-24, lavishes his gifts on the son (a robe, a ring, sandals, a fattened calf) and orders a great celebration.
- Each of us probably has an image in our minds of what God is like. Often we pick up these impressions simply from life experiences, conversations with others or perhaps a church upbringing. But if Jesus is the Christ— the one who speaks and acts for God— his portrait of God is the most important one. According to Jesus, God is a searching, running, embracing,

pardoning, lavishing, partying parent.
- God loves those that deserve his judgement and longs to receive them back. That is why Jesus befriended 'sinners': he wanted to assure them of God's love and convince them to come back to God. That is what his mission as the rescuer was all about.
- The question that emerges for us from all of this is: Are we 'sinners' who are still living at a distance from God, or have we returned to him and sought his forgiveness?

Allow time for questions before wrapping up.

If there is time, you might like to show a section from the Jesus video here— perhaps Jesus' encounter at Simon the Pharisee's house with the sinful woman or his meeting with Zacchaeus. Alternatively, share something of a personal nature about what Jesus' rescue means for you.

Wrap up by reading the Big Idea.

5. The Big Idea

Jesus was God's 'rescuer'. His aim was to find people who have distanced themselves from God and deserve his judgement, and convince them to return home and offer them a fresh start.

6. At Home

For next week please read Luke 20-23 and ask yourself: Why was it necessary for Jesus to die? Note down anything you don't understand, or would like to discuss. We'll have a time for discussion next week.

EXTRA INFORMATION
FOR SESSION THREE

The Comfort and Challenge of God's Judgement

An official doctrine of Jesus' religious contemporaries was that God had set a day at
the end of history when, as the Creator of the world, he would judge every man and
woman for his or her treatment of him and of one another. This is the classic concept
of the 'Judgement Day'—a theme found not only in Judaism, Christianity and Islam, but
also in quite an array of modern films and literature—and it arose directly out of the
religious writings of the Jewish people (the Old Testament) hundreds of years before
Christ. These writings said that just as a diligent parent disciplines a disobedient child,
or a civilised society legislates against law-breakers, so God, because of his diligent
care of humanity would one day deal out his own justice. The reason he didn't punish
until the end of history, so they explained, was to allow people the opportunity to seek
his mercy and mend their ways.

There is a certain comfort and satisfaction in the concept of God's judgement. The
thought that God sees every evil act perpetrated through history—the Jewish holocaust,
Kosovo, East Timor—and that he pledges to bring each one to justice, assures us that
God is not a disinterested observer of the suffering of humanity. He is more like a
caring parent or a just legislator. The Judgement Day, then, is not a theological scare-
tactic designed to make people more religious. It is God's pledge to wounded humanity
that he hears their cries for justice and will one day console them by bringing his
justice to bear on every evil act.

Thus, in a strange sort of way, God's judgement is a consequence of his love. It is
precisely because God loved the victims of the Jewish holocaust that he pledges to punish
the perpetrators of this great evil; it is precisely because he loved the massacred Aboriginal
communities of 19th century Australia that he will vent his anger against those who took
part. As odd as it sounds, the Bible's teaching about divine judgement brings profound
comfort. It reminds us that the Creator hears our cries for justice, and will one day console
us with a display of loving justice the world has never witnessed.

There is another aspect of God's love seen in the concept of the Day of Judgement.
The God of the Bible is to be distinguished from the capricious gods of ancient Greece
or from the strictly just principles of *karma*. He does not 'pay back' every time an
injustice is committed—who of us would be standing if that were the case? Instead,
he mercifully holds off his judgement, allowing ample opportunity for each of us to
experience a spiritual and practical transformation, before he dishes out the full force
of his justice. As one New Testament text states:

But by the same word the heavens and earth that now exist are stored up for fire, being kept until the day of judgement and destruction of the ungodly. But do not overlook this one fact, beloved, that with the Lord one day is as a thousand years, and a thousand years as one day. The Lord is not slow to fulfil his promise as some count slowness, but is patient toward you, not wishing that any should perish, but that all should reach repentance. *(2 Peter 3:7-9)*

There is a less comforting aspect of this idea, of course. God does not see only the great international acts of evil, such as those committed in Auschwitz or on September 11, 2001. He also sees the evil closer to home; in our own country, in our own suburbs, and in our own families. He even sees the injustices of our own hearts. The view of the Old Testament, the view of Jesus himself, was that just as God's love was personal and individual, so his justice would be brought to bear on men and women personally and individually. It is quite an unnerving thought, really! Thus, God's pledge to console us with his justice becomes an exhortation to make use of this merciful interval he has allowed before the last day.

SESSION

4

JESUS' DEATH

1. The Story So Far

Christianity can be summarized as responding appropriately to Jesus Christ.

As the Christ, Jesus possessed the authority of God himself.

Jesus' mission as the rescuer involved finding and rescuing people who had distanced themselves from God.

2. The Last Supper

(read Luke 22:14–20)

Jesus' body and blood sacrificed for us.

3. Tears in the Garden

(read Luke 22:39–46)

Jesus drinks the 'cup' of God's judgement for us.

4. The Criminal, the Christ and the Crucifixion

(read Luke 23:26–46)

Accepting Jesus' authority.
Receiving Jesus' rescue.

5. The Big Idea

The meaning of Jesus' death is simple— Jesus sacrificed his life to take our punishment upon himself, so that we could have open access to God.

6. At Home

Please read the Extra Information for this session. In preparation for next week's session, please read Luke 24.

The Gospel of Luke, Chapters 20-23

Depending on your group's confidence with each other, begin a discussion with the following question: What things do you feel are worth dying for? What makes these things worth dying for?

Alternatively, begin as follows...

1. The Story So Far

- Welcome to Session Four. I hope you found this week's reading interesting and that you've come today/tonight with your questions.
- There have been just three big ideas in the course so far...

Christianity can be summarized as responding appropriately to Jesus Christ.

As the Christ, Jesus possessed the authority of God himself.

Jesus' mission as the rescuer involved finding and rescuing people who had distanced themselves from God.

- As we come to look at Jesus' death, all these ideas come together and reach their climax.
- From the earliest days, the cross was a symbol chosen by Christians to represent the heart of their faith. Whether it be ancient wall paintings or modern jewellery, the cross summarizes the heart of Christian belief.
- This is odd when we think about it,

because the cross is a symbol of execution. It would be like us wearing a noose, or miniature electric chair, around our necks. When we understand the meaning of Jesus' death, however, it makes perfect sense that Christians through the centuries have taken the cross as their symbol.
- So let's look at the events surrounding Jesus' death to find the clues to its meaning. We begin on the Thursday evening before his execution. It is the so-called 'Last Supper'.

2. The Last Supper (read Luke 22:14-20)

Jesus' body and blood sacrificed for us.

- There are many issues we could explore in this passage. Particularly interesting is the fact that Jesus chose to explain his death on the evening of the great Passover meal. The Passover was the high point of the Jewish calendar. It was the night the Jews celebrated God's rescue of the ancient people of Israel. Centuries before Christ, the Jewish people had been held in slavery by the great superpower Egypt. God's judgement eventually fell on the Egyptians and 'passed over' the Jews, who were led out of Egypt via the Red Sea.
- Central to the 'Passover' meal was the killing and eating of a lamb. Some of the blood from the lamb was sprinkled on the door post of each Jewish home. The blood was a sign that the people inside the home were relying on the

mercy of God, confident that God's judgement would pass-over them.

- When Jesus says in verse 20 that his 'blood' is being "poured out for you" he is using this ancient Jewish symbolism to describe his death as a new 'Passover'. His death, then, will be the way in which God's judgement 'passes over' men and women so that they can be forgiven not condemned.
- After this meal, Jesus takes his disciples on an evening stroll through a well known public garden. The reality of Jesus' impending sacrifice now powerfully begins to affect him...

3. Tears in the Garden (read Luke 22:39–46)

Jesus drinks the 'cup' of God's judgement for us.

- This is an unusual insight into Jesus. At every point throughout his life he has been totally in control. But now, on the night before his death, he appears to be overwhelmed by his circumstances.
- Strangely, in verse 42 he describes his torment as a "cup". What is this "cup" that could trouble someone of such authority?
- Again, ancient symbolism helps make it clear. In the ancient world, one common way to assassinate people (kings or whomever) was to poison their cup. From this, the phrase 'to drink the cup' became a metaphor for tragedy or disaster.
- In the Jewish Scriptures (the Old Testament), this same metaphor was often used to describe the tragedy or disaster that God brought on nations and individuals as punishment for their evil actions. In other words, the 'cup' became a symbol of God's just punishment. To offer just one example:

Jeremiah 25:15-29 (600 BC):
Thus the LORD, the God of Israel, said to me: "Take from my hand this cup of the wine of wrath, and make all the nations to whom I send you drink it. So I took the cup from the LORD's hand, and made all the nations to whom the LORD sent me drink it: ...to make them a desolation and a waste, a hissing and a curse... 'Thus says the LORD of hosts: You must drink!... You shall not go unpunished..."

- It is this 'cup' of judgement that Jesus is about to drink. But Jesus will drink the cup of God's judgement, not for his own wrongdoing, but for ours. As we said earlier in the evening, his blood was to be "poured out for you."

You can use the 'telephone book illustration' at this point, as follows. Imagine that the light [point to the light in your lounge-room] represents God. My empty right hand is me, wanting to enjoy God's light and warmth [raise empty right hand towards light]. But God knows that we have all sinned and done wrong. Imagine a telephone book in which God has listed all our sins and disobedience [put telephone book on right hand]. The book stands between us and God, preventing us from having a relationship with him. Because of his love, God sent Jesus into the world [your empty left hand]. Unlike anyone else who ever lived, Jesus had no record of sins against his name. By his death, all our sin and judgement is transferred onto Jesus [transfer book to left hand]. Now we are free to have access to God, because we are now free from the punishment that our sins deserve [empty right hand raised towards light].

- With all this in mind, let's look at the death of Jesus itself...

4. The Criminal, the Christ and the Crucifixion (read Luke 23:26–46)

- There are many important things to note in this passage, but Jesus' conversation with the criminal dying beside him deserves our special attention. It takes us to the heart of Luke's Gospel, and therefore to the heart of Christianity.
- The two main ideas of Luke's Gospel reach their climax in this scene...

Accepting Jesus' authority

- One of the striking aspects of this passage is the way everyone seems to reject Jesus' authority—in verse 35 the Jewish rulers reject him (read it); in verses 36-37 the Roman soldiers reject him (read it); and then in verse 39 one of the criminals also rejects him (read it).
- The dying man on the other side of

Jesus, however, does not reject Jesus. Instead, he recognizes what everyone else failed to recognize—Jesus is God's appointed king. In verse 42 he addresses Jesus as the one who rules God's "kingdom": "Remember me when you come into your kingdom" (read it).

- This, in a sense, is the real climax of Luke's story of Jesus—Jesus is the Christ, whose authority we should recognize.
- The second big idea of Luke's Gospel is also prominent in this passage...

Receiving Jesus' rescue

- Jesus' acceptance of this man is instant and unconditional. In verse 43 Jesus makes the bold promise that this man, despite his previous wrongs, will be with Jesus in the kingdom of God, or "paradise" (read it).
- Here is one of the clearest examples of Jesus' mission—a criminal lost from God, but now found and restored to God the moment he realizes that Jesus is the one with the authority to rescue him.
- We should remember that the only reason the criminal could be rescued was because Jesus soon drank the 'cup' of punishment that this man (and all of us) deserved. He was the means of our own Passover. To put it bluntly— the only reason any of us can get 'off the hook' is because Jesus was put on the hook for us (read verses 44-46).
- Actually, this theme is clear in the prophecy about the coming of Christ written centuries before Christ. If you

could go back to the Extra Information sheet from Session Two and turn to the last passage (p.49; p.21 in Guest's Manual), I'd like to read it to you. When we hold in mind that this was written around 700BC the passage is quite extraordinary. (Now read Isaiah 52:13–53:12 from the Extra Information for Session Two.)

Allow time for questions before concluding.

Wrap up by reading The Big Idea.

5. The Big Idea

The meaning of Jesus' death is simple— Jesus sacrificed his life to take our punishment upon himself, so that we could have open access to God.

6. At Home

Please read the other Extra Information for this session. In preparation for next week's session, please read Luke 24.

EXTRA INFORMATION FOR SESSION FOUR

Jesus and the Rescue of God

Two themes have weaved their way through the whole of Luke's account of Jesus. The first is Jesus' status over us as the Christ. The second is Jesus' mission for us as the Rescuer. Both themes are drawn together brilliantly in the account of Jesus' final moment.

After a sleepless night, two spurious legal trials and a series of public beatings and floggings, Jesus is led, carrying a large wooden beam, outside the city boundary to a rocky outcrop called 'the Place of the Skull'. There, along with two other criminals, Jesus is strapped and nailed to a cross-like structure. A crowd, perhaps in their hundreds, gathers to witness the end of an extraordinary life.

There are two stark ironies running through the account. Everyone there that day rejected Jesus' claim to be God's king, or Christ: the leaders who organised the death sentence, the soldiers who carried it out, and one of the criminals who hung next to him. They all saw Jesus hanging there naked, bleeding and dying, looking rather unkingly, and mocked him with words to the effect of, "If you're meant to be the Christ/King, do something!" But the irony is this: what everyone else rejected that day, the second criminal came to believe, namely, that Jesus is the king of God's kingdom. His words make this clear: "Jesus, remember me when you come into your **king**dom."

In these words, the first major theme of Luke's biography reaches another climax. Men and women ought to acknowledge the authority of Jesus as the Christ.

The second irony is even more startling. Everyone who yelled abuse at Jesus that day assumed that if he were the Christ he would rescue himself. The leaders sneered, "Let him rescue himself"; the soldiers yelled "Rescue yourself"; and the criminal then added, "Rescue yourself and us". They figured that surely the person who was meant to speak and act for the Creator couldn't possibly wind up in such tragic circumstances. But they had failed to realise that this was exactly what the Christ had come to do. He had no intention of rescuing himself from the cross because his mission was precisely to rescue others by that cross. For on the cross he would drink the cup of judgement we deserve so that those who return to God would be rescued.

This point is skilfully emphasized in Luke's description of the second criminal. He refused to join in the insults. Instead, realising Jesus' authority he pleaded with him for a place in his Kingdom. No sooner had he said, "please remember me", than Jesus responded with words of total acceptance: "...you will be with me in Paradise". The criminal had found his rescue.

In these words, the second major theme of Luke's biography reaches a climax. Through Jesus Christ, men and women can find rescue from God's judgement.

God the Rescuer

The events of Jesus' final 24 hours not only underline the heroism of Jesus himself, but they also speak volumes about the Creator. The story of the Christ is really a story about the God whose work and passion he personified. As God's representative on earth, Jesus knew all along that his words and actions provided the world with glimpses into God's own character. His teaching made God's voice heard; his healings displayed God's passion for our welfare; his forgiveness mirrored God's mercy; his command 'follow me' pointed ultimately to God's leadership.

But more than this, although only implicit in Luke's Gospel, other New Testament texts (notably the Gospel of John) make clear that Christ not only 'represented' God, in the sense of being the one appointed to speak and act on his behalf, but he actually 'embodied' the presence of God himself. It turns out that the reason Jesus of Nazareth could hand out God's words, God's healing and God's forgiveness is that God himself dwelt fully within him.

Christ's divinity—his embodiment of God—is, in my opinion, most profoundly and beautifully expressed in his death on the cross. There, in the bitter-sweet climax of Jesus' life, God himself makes known to the world the desperate lengths to which he is willing to go in order to rescue us from the judgement we deserve. The very name 'Jesus'—which as I mentioned earlier means literally 'God rescues'—turns out to be not just a vague statement about an aloof God's intentions to rescue people, but a personal pledge about his own costly involvement in our rescue on the cross.

Thus, in the man who was willing to die for us we actually discover the God who is anxious to rescue us. It is not hard, in light of this, to understand why the cross very quickly became the most recognisable symbol of the Christian faith.

SESSION

5

JESUS, HERE AND NOW

1. The Story So Far

Christianity can be summarized as responding appropriately to Jesus Christ.

As the Christ, Jesus possessed the authority of God himself.

Jesus' mission as the rescuer involved finding and rescuing people who had distanced themselves from God.

Jesus willingly sacrificed his life to take upon himself the judgement we deserve.

2. The Meaning of Jesus' Resurrection

Clue one: a supernatural body (read Luke 24:30-43).
Clue two: elevation to God's right hand (read Luke 22:66-69).

3. Our Response

(read Luke 24:44-47)

a) Since Jesus is God's powerful, ruling Christ (Messiah), the only appropriate response is *repentance*, a turnaround of attitude that accepts Christ's leadership of our lives.

b) Since Jesus is the Rescuer who died for us, repentant people are now able to receive God's *forgiveness*.

4. The Big Idea

The fact that Jesus has been raised from the dead demands that we respond to him. Jesus expected this response to take the form of repentance and seeking forgiveness.

5. At Home

Please take time to fill out the questionnaire and return it to us as soon as convenient. More importantly, take time to consider your own response to Jesus. If you want to be a Christian, why not tell God? The following prayer is not a magical set of words, but it may help you express to God your desire to be a Christian.

> Lord,
> Thank you for Jesus, your Christ: for his life, death and resurrection.
> I admit that I have sinned against you and lived at a distance from you.
> I am truly sorry.
> Because of Jesus, please forgive me.
> Help me, from this time on, to see things your way and to live accordingly.
> Thank you. Amen.

The Gospel of Luke, Chapter 24

1. The Story So Far

- Welcome to the Final Session. I hope you found this week's reading interesting and that you've come today/tonight with your questions.
- There have been four related ideas in the course so far...

Christianity can be summarized as responding appropriately to Jesus Christ.

As the Christ, Jesus possessed the authority of God himself.

Jesus' mission as the rescuer involved finding and rescuing people who had distanced themselves from God.

Jesus willingly sacrificed his life to take upon himself the judgement we deserve.

- If Luke (and the other Gospel writers) had finished the story of Jesus with his death, we might have concluded that Jesus was another of the great martyrs of history who died for worthy causes. However, all the Gospels are emphatic that the story did not end with Jesus' death. They insist that he was raised to life again a few days later.
- If the resurrection were essentially untrue, this would rob the whole story of Jesus of credibility. It would turn Jesus into a lovely mythical character such as Santa.
- However, if true, the resurrection turns Jesus into far more than a great martyr

from the past. It puts Jesus in a league of his own. The Extra Information for Session Five explores the historicity of the resurrection and shows that one must have very good reasons for not accepting the event as true.
- Tonight/today, however, we're going to focus on the meaning of the resurrection. Because this is not merely an event of history, it is an event with significance here and now.

2. The Meaning of Jesus' Resurrection

- There are two clues in the account to the significance of Jesus' resurrection. The first is a quite obvious one as you read through the narrative. After the resurrection, Jesus' body is somehow changed.

Clue one: a supernatural body (read Luke 24:30-43).

- On the one hand, Jesus' body is perfectly natural. In verse 39 he insists he is not a mere 'ghost' and in verses 42-43 he eats some food to prove it.
- But, on the other hand, something is physically different about his body. In verse 31 he disappears from sight right before the eyes of his disciples. And in verse 36 he suddenly appears again before the disciples.
- The fact that such appearing and disappearing occurs nowhere else in Luke's account implies that a change has occurred in Jesus. The resurrection

is not the mere *resuscitation* of Jesus, it is his *elevation* to a new reality.

- Put another way, in the resurrection Jesus is not merely returned to his former glory, he is exalted to a new kind of glory. In fact, earlier in the chapter (in verse 26), Jesus described his resurrection reality as his 'glory' (read verses 25-26).
- So what exactly is this new 'glory'? Jesus answered that question in a statement he made at his trial three days earlier. This is the second clue.

Clue two: elevation to God's right hand (read Luke 22:66-69).

- At his trial Jesus makes the startling claim that death would not be the end of his majesty. It would, in fact, be a doorway into a greater majesty. In the words of verse 69, after his death he would be "seated at God's right hand of power".
- Sitting at God's "right hand" is a metaphor; it's like talking about your 'right hand man'. It indicates that after his death, Jesus would share in God's rule of the world.
- The resurrection is the doorway into this reality.
- In the resurrection Jesus is elevated from a temporary, local authority to an authority that is permanent and universal. He is not only the Jewish Messiah of the first century; he is God's appointed king of the world for the 21st century as well.
- That is what the resurrection of Jesus is all about.

Perhaps field questions for a moment about the meaning of the resurrection. Then say...

- If Jesus has been raised from death (to "sit at God's right hand") it means that he is not just a fascinating story from the past but an exciting reality for the present. This means we need to start thinking about what this might mean for us today.

3. Our Response (read Luke 24:44–47)

- Fortunately, we don't have to speculate about what Jesus thought was the appropriate response to his life, death and resurrection. By instructing his disciples about what exactly they were to offer to the world, Jesus makes clear what he expects of people like us who have heard the news about him.
- That expectation is captured in the two key words in verse 47—'repentance' and 'forgiveness'.
- Just as there are two aspects to Jesus' life (his authority as the Christ and his mission as the Rescuer), so there are two aspects to our response.

a) Since Jesus is God's powerful, ruling Christ (Messiah), the only appropriate response is repentance, a turnaround of attitude that accepts Christ's leadership of our lives.

- Unfortunately, for some of us the word 'repent' in verse 46 has bad connotations. It reminds us of an angry preacher telling us to be good or we'll go to hell. But what Jesus said here is quite different.

- To 'repent' means to stop going in one direction, to turn around, and to go in a completely new direction. The prodigal son of chapter 15 (Session 3) is a great example of repentance—he journeyed a long way from his father, but he had a change of heart. He turned round and headed home.

- You can see this in the Greek word that we translate 'repentance'. It is *metanoia*—'meta' means change and 'noia' means mind. Repentance is a complete change of mind and attitude. Jesus is calling for a new mindset that accepts his authority (as the Christ) over our lives.

- This is very important to understand, because Jesus is not primarily asking for us to pull up our socks and be good. If he had meant that, he could have said *metamorphosis*, which means a change of form or action.

- Of course, a changed attitude will undoubtedly lead to a changed lifestyle, but it must begin with the mindset.

- There is a second aspect to responding to Jesus and it corresponds to the second major theme of Luke's Gospel...

b) Since Jesus is the Rescuer who died for us, repentant people are now able to receive God's forgiveness.

- Part of turning back to God in repentance is acknowledging that we've behaved badly towards him, that we have sinned and need his forgiveness.

- Because Jesus' death absorbs our punishment (remember the phone book illustration?), we can turn back to God and ask his forgiveness for all our wrongs, and be confident that he will forgive us.

- Receiving God's rescue is not a matter of working hard at being good or religious. It is about God forgiving us for all our wrongs because Jesus died on our behalf.

- Of course, this doesn't mean we are free to go out and sin all we like. This would be clear evidence that we have not experienced a 'change of mind' (repentance) in the first place. But it does mean we can each live our lives as best we can, confident that despite our many failures God accepts us and has forgiven us.

Allow time for questions.

Also, share something personal about your faith. In particular, indicate how 'repentance' and 'forgiveness' determine the shape of the whole Christian life (not just how one becomes a Christian). Explain how you are constantly seeing things differently because of God and trying to live accordingly (i.e., 'change of mind' or 'repentance'), and how despite your failure always to live God's way you are confident of God's forgiveness (because of Jesus).

4. The Big Idea

The fact that Jesus has been raised from the dead demands that we respond to him. Jesus expected this response to take the form of repentance and seeking forgiveness.

Make special comment about the homework. Urge them to think seriously about repenting and asking God for his forgiveness, if they haven't already. Also, talk them through the prayer at the end of the outline.

Some leaders may wish to pray through the prayer on the night, giving people an opportunity to become Christians then and there. Alternatively (or as well), you may prefer to follow through with each group member individually to see where they are up to.

Also, remind your group about any follow-up course your church offers.

5. At Home

Please take time to fill out the questionnaire and return it to us as soon as convenient. More importantly, take time to consider your own response to Jesus. If you want to be a Christian, why not tell God? The following prayer is not a magical set of words, but it may help you express to God your desire to be a Christian.

Lord,
Thank you for Jesus, your Christ: for his life, death and resurrection.
I admit that I have sinned against you and lived at a distance from you.
I am truly sorry.
Because of Jesus, please forgive me.
Help me, from this time on, to see things your way and to live accordingly.
Thank you. Amen.

EXTRA INFORMATION
FOR SESSION FIVE

The Resurrection of Christ

In the past, people have tried to rule out the entire discussion about 'resurrection' as absurd. They have said, "In our consistent human experience, dead people just do not come back to life. Therefore, Jesus could not have been raised from the dead either." That is, because we have never seen a resurrection, we rule it out as a possibility. This 'logic' was most forcefully stated by the renowned 18th century English philosopher, David Hume. He argued that our solid 'background evidence' about the reliability of the laws of nature should override all 'foreground claims' about the abrogation of those laws, or 'miracles'. At first, this seems reasonable. The fact that I've never seen a pink and polka dot coloured elephant, combined with the fact that I know they consistently come in gray, would make me extremely sceptical if anyone claimed to have seen such a creature.

However, there are a number of holes in Hume's argument, as many modern philosophers have been keen to point out.[†] Human observation, whether personal or scientific, does not establish in full the fixity of natural laws. For example, if you lived in England two centuries ago, you would have been brought up to believe that all swans were white. You would have dismissed the rumours about black swans (coming from Southern Hemisphere countries like Australia and South Africa) as hoaxes or a case of mistaken identity. But the fact of the matter is that black swans did exist, even though the English had never seen them. Limited observation can only tell you what to predict, not what actually is. So, an 18th century Englishman could not rightly say, "I have never seen a black swan, therefore they do not exist". He could only say, "The evidence available to me leads me to expect that black swans do not exist".

Thus, the critical issue is **evidence**. There is no disputing that in our experience resurrections from the dead do not happen. But this alone cannot rule out a resurrection on a particular occasion. The question must be asked: Is the 'foreground evidence' about Jesus' resurrection sufficient to challenge, or at least create an exception to, the 'background evidence' concerning the normal function (or rather non-function) of a dead body? In other words, is evidence for Jesus rising from the dead strong enough to contradict our expectation that such things do not happen?

I think there are four pieces of evidence that suggest Jesus was raised from the dead. I'll present each of them and then raise some arguments against them. You can be the judge of whether or not the evidence is strong.

† For instance, see the article by the Oxford University Professor of Philosophy, Richard Swinburne: R. Swinburne, 'Evidence for the Resurrection', in *The Resurrection: An Interdisciplinary Symposium on the Resurrection of Jesus*, Oxford University Press, Oxford, 1998, pp. 191-212.

EVIDENCE ONE: **Jesus' tomb was corpse-less.**
One of the most compelling arguments for Jesus' resurrection is the fact that it is almost beyond doubt that Jesus' tomb was empty a short time after his execution.

There are three things that put the empty tomb beyond reasonable doubt.

REASON ONE: **Jesus' resurrection was proclaimed in Jerusalem just weeks after the crucifixion.**
This is very important. If Jesus' tomb was not empty, such preaching could not have taken place. The tomb was owned by a prominent politician of the time named Joseph of Arimathea and so could easily be found by anyone who wanted to know. How on earth would the apostles have gotten away with telling people in Jerusalem (where Jesus was buried) that they had seen Jesus alive and well, without a body being produced to contradict them? Let me put it like this. Down at Balmoral Beach in Mosman, Sydney, there is a statue of a dog named 'Billy'. He was a well-known canine in the area years ago. Suppose next week I claim to have seen the statue of Billy the wonder dog come to life and run away. Now, I might just get away with that claim in Perth, New Zealand or Wales (no offence intended), where no-one could check up on me. But I couldn't get away with it in Mosman itself. Mosman residents could too easily take a drive down to the beach and prove me a liar. The fact is, the first public claim of Jesus' resurrection occurred less than five kilometres from his burial site. This is a strong reason for believing that the tomb was, in fact, empty.

REASON TWO: **Jesus' tomb did not become a holy site in the years immediately after his death.**
This doesn't sound very interesting on its own, I know. But what is odd, is that during the time of Jesus there were at least 50 tombs of great Jewish religious leaders in Palestine, and all of these sites were considered to be holy sites. A fair bit of religious activity took place at them. So, the question needs to be asked: If Jesus' corpse remained in the tomb, why was this custom not followed?

REASON THREE: **The Jewish leaders did not contest the empty tomb.**
In Matthew's biography, it is clear that the popular argument against Jesus' resurrection in the years following the claim did not revolve around whether the tomb was empty, but how it became empty. It was assumed, even by those who violently opposed the disciples' claim, that the tomb of Jesus was vacant and had been from a couple of days after his execution. There's even an ancient document a hundred years after Matthew's Gospel that records a debate between a Jewish intellectual named Trypho and a Christian leader named Justin. In the document, it is clear the Jews of that time still did not argue against the tomb being empty. They simply raised suspicion about how it came to be empty!

So the obvious question is, "How did the tomb come to be empty?" Here are a few possible explanations.

COUNTER-ARGUMENT ONE: Perhaps Jesus didn't die on the cross, but simply fell unconscious, was buried, and later got better in the tomb.
According to this explanation, Jesus unwrapped his own burial clothes, rolled away the boulder that blocked the entrance, walked for two or three kilometres, showed himself to his friends and was somehow able to convince them that God had powerfully raised him to a new life. All I can say to this explanation is that it used to be argued. Modern scholars are now embarrassed that this argument was ever raised. The more we've learnt about Roman execution practices in the period, the more implausible it looks that Jesus 'got better' in the tomb, let alone convinced his friends that he was powerfully alive and well.

COUNTER-ARGUMENT TWO: Perhaps they went to the wrong tomb on Sunday morning.
Jesus' tomb was visited by some women who were his followers. They were the ones who discovered the tomb was empty. Some people have suggested they visited the wrong tomb.

This explanation surmises that the tomb Mary and the other women visited looked like the one Jesus had been placed in, but in actual fact was another one that happened to be unused. Thus, the whole of Christianity is based on a couple of people losing their way in the night. This explanation faces the very serious problem that sooner or later someone would have checked again. Remember, the tomb where Jesus was buried was owned by one of the prominent politicians of the time. It could easily have been accessed and the women's mistake would have been revealed.

COUNTER-ARGUMENT THREE: Perhaps the disciples stole the body.
This is the oldest explanation of the empty tomb (actually the second oldest behind the claim that he was, in fact, raised!). It's the one Jewish people have used ever since the 1st century. For me, though, it is also the hardest to accept. Think of it this way. Suppose I stand up in church next week and claim to have seen the statue of 'Billy' the wonder dog come to life and run away. After a thorough search of Balmoral Beach, it is discovered that the statue is missing. Within weeks I'm a national celebrity. A radio talk-show host invites me onto his show and praises me for having seen a modern miracle. TV current affairs reporters ring me offering a million dollar contract for the exclusive rights to a step-by-step re-enactment of the miracle. Media moguls want to publish my story, and Oxford University invites me for a lecture tour. What would you conclude? I'm sure some of you would be thinking, "I bet he stole the statue for his own personal gain". That's what I would conclude too.

But suppose things went the other way, and I had nothing to gain by my lie. The talk-show host grills me for being a scam artist. The reporters expose me as a fraud. My family disowns me. The media mogul prints an article about the stupidity of my belief. I am eventually taken to court and tried for 'public deception', and then taken to prison until I admit to the truth. If I had stolen the statue, how long do you think it would take before I confessed to my deception? Not long I think.

The same problem applies to Jesus' resurrection. If the disciples had become rich and famous for their claims about Jesus, it would be easier to conclude that they stole the body from the tomb and made up this incredible resurrection story. But the opposite is true. They were considered 'heretics' and 'traitors' by many of their fellow Jews. They were taken to court and thrown in prison. And many of them were, in fact, executed (for the names, dates and methods of execution for some of these eyewitness, see page 207 of my book, *Simply Christianity: A modern guide to the ancient faith*). Why, if they knew they had merely taken the body from the tomb, did they die for the claim that Jesus was raised from the tomb? It is true that plenty of people throughout history have suffered and died for beliefs they did not know were wrong, but who on earth would willingly die for something they knew was a lie? It is an extremely difficult historical and psychological question to answer without a resurrection.

In my opinion, none of these attempts to explain away the empty tomb succeeds. This brings me back to my first piece of evidence. It seems beyond reasonable doubt that the tomb of Jesus was actually corpse-less on Easter Sunday morning, and no attempt to explain it away satisfies the facts.

Let me offer a few more pieces of evidence for the resurrection of Jesus.

EVIDENCE TWO: **Women were the first witnesses to the resurrection.**
One of the interesting features of the biographies of Jesus is that they all claim that women were the first people to witness the event. This may not sound like a very big deal to modern readers, but in 1st century Palestine it was a very significant point. A woman's testimony was considered untrustworthy by 1st century Jewish leaders, so much so that they were not allowed to give evidence in a court of law. So, for instance, first century Jewish historian Josephus writes about certain requirements in court:

> But let not a single witness be credited, but three, or two at the least, and those such whose testimony is confirmed by their good lives. But let not the testimony of women be admitted, on account of the frivolity and boldness of their sex. Nor let servants be admitted to give testimony, on account of the ignobility of their soul.
>
> Josephus, *The Antiquities of the Jews*, Book 4, chapter 8

I know this sounds incredibly unjust, but I raise this only to illustrate the legal situation of the time (incidentally, the fact that women were the first to witness the resurrection shows that God had no problem with their testimony).

So, if you were making up a story about a resurrection and you wanted your fellow 1st century Jews to believe it, why would you include women as the initial witnesses, unless of course it just happened to be embarrassingly true? All four biographies agree that women were the first to witness Jesus' resurrection.

EVIDENCE THREE: Similarities and dissimilarities in the accounts.
Like police assessing the evidence of witnesses, historians look not only for general agreement between various accounts of a particular event (convergence) but also for small individual variations (divergence). The slight divergence tells you the witnesses haven't simply copied each other's stories.

The Gospels live up to this convergence/divergence test. On the one hand, the different accounts agree in profound ways. For example, they agree on the day it occurred and that it was morning when it happened. They agree that women were the first to realise the resurrection had taken place. And they agree that there was confusion and doubt among the apostles when they first heard that Jesus was raised. However, someone could look at all this 'agreement' and argue that the biographers just got together and made sure they all said the same thing. But the reality is there are also significant differences between the biographies. And some of these differences are very difficult (though not impossible) to reconcile with each other. For example, Mark's biography says that just after daylight on Sunday morning, three women first went to the tomb. John's biography, however, mentions only one woman, and she apparently visited while it was still dark.

My point is, if all the accounts were full of contradictions you could conclude they were not trustworthy. But if they were identical, word for word, you could conclude there was a planned scam or cover-up. But neither looks likely. The different biographies display both profound agreement and significant variation.

EVIDENCE FOUR: Transformation of the disciples.
A fourth piece of evidence for the resurrection is the amazing transformation of Jesus' disciples after Easter Sunday. How did a small group of uneducated Jewish people become so adamant about their leader's resurrection that they confidently claimed, proclaimed, debated, stood trial, suffered and, in some cases, died, for that claim? And how on earth did devout 1st century Jews (who naturally avoided other races and nations) begin the largest, most international and multicultural religion in the world?

Let me give you an individual example of the transformation that took place in one of Jesus' followers. In the biographies, it is clear that Jesus' own brothers did not believe in him. In fact, according to Mark's biography, early on, they thought their famous brother was insane. However, in the Bible book called 'Acts', which describes the first years of the church after Jesus' resurrection, one of Jesus' brothers, James, has become a key leader of the early church. And, as you may remember from earlier in the book, the Jewish historian in this period, Josephus, even records something about James we don't hear about in the Bible—that he was eventually executed for his belief in his older brother. How did this happen? What stands between the unbelief of James recorded in the biographies and his willingness to be executed for believing in the risen Jesus? What caused such a transformation if it was not that he had seen his brother raised from death? This is only one example. Several, if not most, of the first apostles were eventually executed for their belief in the risen Jesus. What caused such fearless devotion?

Over the years, there have been a number of attempts to explain away this transformation. Here are a few of them.

COUNTER-ARGUMENT ONE: **Perhaps Jesus' disciples were inclined toward belief in resurrection.**

One explanation has suggested that Jesus' followers were already theologically biased toward believing in resurrections, and so it would not have taken very much for them to think that their beloved teacher was alive.

The first version of this explanation insists they were influenced by the *common Jewish belief that the dead can be raised.* But this is plainly wrong. There were two schools of thought in Jewish society at this time and neither believed in the type of resurrection the apostles claimed about Jesus. Sadducees (the ruling class of Israel) denied any possibility of resurrection. As far as they were concerned, when you're dead, you're dead. The Pharisees (a large sect of strict Jews) on the other hand did believe in resurrection from the dead. However, they believed there was one resurrection only, and that this event occurred for all of humanity at the end of history—the day of judgement. As far as we know, the claim of a solo resurrection in history was not, for Jews of this time, part of their world-view.

So, when the disciples came out saying they had seen Jesus raised from the dead, they were not showing their Jewish influences at all. They were, in fact, defying those influences. Their claim was as strange and unique in their day as it is in ours. As Dr. A. E. McGrath of Oxford University, says:

> The history of Israel is littered with the corpses of pious Jewish martyrs, none of whom were ever thought of as having been raised from the dead in such a manner.
>
> A. E. McGrath, *Bridge-building*, IVP, Leicester, 1992, p.162

Others attribute the disciples 'bias' toward belief in resurrection to *Greek myths about dying and rising gods.* It is true there are stories in Greek mythology which centre around gods who die and rise again, but these are presented *as* myths. They are written in the literary style of mythology, and have no historical placement or appeal to eyewitnesses. To quote McGrath again:

> ...there are no known instances of this myth being applied to any specific historical figure in pagan literature...the New Testament documents with some care give the place and the date of both the death and the resurrection of Jesus, as well as identifying the witnesses to both. (pp.162-163)

In addition to this, according to the Greek philosophical view of the universe at this time, a resurrection involving a *real physical body* that could be touched, and that could eat, was absurd. But this is exactly what the apostles claimed. In fact, their claim was occasionally rejected by Greeks precisely because of this contradiction between Greek thought and the disciples' claim. Furthermore, it must be remembered that all of Jesus' disciples were Palestinian Jews. To them, Greek religious myths were blasphemous. To suggest that their central message came from such Greek myths is unlikely in the extreme, and very few historians today pursue this line of argument.

There are no reasons for thinking the disciples were favourably disposed or biased toward belief in Jesus' resurrection. If anything, their influences ran against such a claim, and yet they still made it.

COUNTER-ARGUMENT TWO: **Perhaps the disciples simply saw a 'vision'.**
Some people have suggested that what the apostles saw was not the raised body of Jesus, but some religious vision, like the kind spoken of in many religions. The basic problem with this explanation is that the Bible is full of 'visions' and is happy to name them as such. There is no question that the eyewitnesses (and biographers) of Jesus' resurrection knew the difference between a vision and a real event. However, nowhere do they speak of the resurrection as a vision. People who suggest the resurrection was simply a religious vision are left with a dilemma: why did people who were well acquainted with visions claim that the resurrection was a real physical event?

COUNTER-ARGUMENT THREE: **Perhaps the disciples hallucinated.**
Another explanation of the disciples' transformation suggests that after their terrible weekend—seeing their master executed, not sleeping or eating—the disciples may well have experienced hallucinations of Jesus which they thought were real. The problem with this explanation is that, to sane people, even hallucinations are clearly identifiable as such after the event. Secondly, you have the problem of explaining how over 500 people in many settings could have had the same hallucination over a forty day period.

This transformation of the disciples is so difficult to explain that a leading ancient historian from Germany, Dr Pinchas Lapide, has admitted that Jesus' resurrection must have occurred. This is not so amazing by itself—many modern scholars believe Jesus rose from the dead. What is amazing is that Lapide is a devout Jew who adamantly opposes the Christian belief that Jesus was the Christ. Here is what he concludes:

> How was it possible that his disciples, who by no means excelled in intelligence, eloquence, or strength of faith, were able to begin their victorious march of conversion...? In a purely logical analysis, the resurrection of Jesus is 'the lesser of two evils' for all those who seek a rational explanation of the worldwide consequences of that Easter faith. Thus according to my opinion, the resurrection belongs to the category of the truly real...
>
> *The Resurrection of Jesus: a Jewish perspective*, SPCK, London, 1984

Conclusion

More could be said on this topic. For example, another obvious line of argument that contributes to the believability of the resurrection is the very existence of God. Put simply, if there is a God, raising someone from the dead would hardly be a difficult thing to pull off. The fact that 80% of Australians believe in the existence of God means that, for at least 14 million of us, the resurrection of a person claiming to be God's agent on earth should not be dismissed simply because resurrections don't normally occur. If the historical evidence points decisively in the direction of Jesus really rising from the dead, then our belief in the existence of an all-powerful Creator, who can do things like raise the dead, gets us philosophically over the line, and right between the posts!

Of course, if you don't believe in the existence of God, this piece of philosophical argumentation is of no value for you. But you are still left with the very difficult task of explaining how, historically speaking, it looks as though a man who said he would rise from the dead, did.

Let me close by recounting an interesting debate.

On May 2nd and 3rd 1985, the philosophy faculty of Liberty University, Virginia USA, hosted a professionally adjudicated debate between the renowned scholar and atheist, Prof. Antony Flew, and an internationally recognised expert in the origins of Christianity, historian, Dr Gary Habermas. The topic of the debate was "The Historicity of the Resurrection: Did Jesus Rise from the Dead?" It was attended by 3000 people, and the transcripts of the debate have since been published as a book.[†]

Two panels of judges were employed for the debate. One consisted of five professional debate judges who were asked to judge "the argumentation technique of the debaters". The second panel consisted of five academic philosophers who were instructed "to judge the content of the debate and render a winner". All ten judges serve on the faculties of leading American universities and represented a wide spectrum of views and persuasions.

The panel of professional adjudicators, judging argumentation, voted three to two in favour of Habermas. The panel of philosophers, judging content, cast four votes for Habermas and the fifth deemed the debate a draw. Overall, then, the debate was won convincingly seven to two (with one draw), in favour of the affirmative, that Jesus was raised from the dead.

Of course, this does not prove the resurrection. I refer to this important debate merely to point out that belief in the resurrection of Jesus is far from ridiculous. Despite our quite reasonable expectation (based on the 'background evidence' of the reliability of the laws of nature) that dead people do not come back to life, there is good 'foreground evidence' leading intelligent people to believe that an exception to the norm has occurred in the case of Christ; that 36 hours after his execution he was raised to life.

---

†   G. Habermas and A. Flew, *Did Jesus Rise from the Dead: The Resurrection Debate*, Harper and Row, San Fransisco, 1987.

THE GOSPEL OF LUKE

Chapter 1[†]

Dedication: to Theophilus[††]

[1] Since many have attempted to put together an account of the things that have been fulfilled among us [2] (just as these things were passed on to us by those who from the beginning were eyewitnesses and guardians of the message), [3] so it seemed good to me as well, having checked everything very carefully from the start, to write something orderly for you, Your Excellency, Theophilus. [4] My aim is that you may know the reliability of the reports you have heard.

The Births of John and Jesus

[5] In the time of Herod, King of Judea, there was a certain priest called Zechariah from the priestly division of Abijah. He had a wife, Elizabeth, who was descended from the line of Aaron. [6] They were both righteous people before God, living blamelessly according to all the commands and righteous ways of the Lord. [7] Yet they had no children, because Elizabeth was barren; and they were both well advanced in age.

[8] Now it happened that Zechariah's division was rostered to perform the priestly duties before God, [9] and according to the custom of the priesthood, he was allotted the task of going into the temple of the Lord to burn incense. [10] A large crowd outside the temple was praying at the time the incense was burned.

[11] An angelic Messenger* of the Lord appeared to him, standing at the right of the incense altar, [12] and when he saw this, Zechariah was very troubled and afraid.

[13] The Messenger said to him, "Do not be afraid, Zechariah, because your prayers have been heard—your wife Elizabeth will bear you a son, and you are to give him the name John. [14] He will be a joy and a delight to you, and many will rejoice because of his birth, [15] for he will be great before the Lord. He will not drink wine or strong drink, and he will be filled with the Holy Spirit, even from his mother's womb. [16] He will turn many of the sons of Israel back to the Lord their God, [17] and he will go before the Lord in the spirit and power of Elijah, to turn the hearts of fathers to their children, and to turn the disobedient to the wise way of the righteous. He will prepare a people who are ready for the Lord."

[18] Zechariah said to the Messenger, "How will I know this is true? For I am an old man and my wife is advanced in age."

[19] The Messenger replied, "I am Gabriel who stands in the presence of God. I was sent to speak to you, and make this important announcement to you. [20] But now you will be silent and not able to speak until the day these things come about, because you did not believe my message, which will be fulfilled in due course."

[21] While all this was happening, the people were waiting for Zechariah, and wondered why he was taking so long in the temple. [22] When he came out, he was completely unable to speak to them, and they realised that he had seen a vision in the temple. He was making signs to them, and remained speechless.

[23] Eventually, the time of Zechariah's service came to an end, and he went home. [24] After this, Elizabeth his wife became pregnant. She hid herself for five months, and her comment was, [25] "So this is how the Lord has acted for me, when he looked kindly on me, and took away my disgrace among the people".

[26] In the sixth month, the angel Gabriel was sent from God to a city in Galilee called Nazareth, [27] to a virgin who was engaged to a man named Joseph. Joseph was from the family line of

---

†   The chapter divisions and subheadings are not part of the original Greek text of Luke. They have been added for ease of reading and reference.

††   Many ancient pieces of literature were dedicated to important individuals, often the sponsor of the work.

*   Traditionally, *angel*; also below.

David, and the virgin's name was Mary. [28] The angelic Messenger went to her and said, "Rejoice, O highly favoured one, the Lord is with you".

[29] But when she heard this, Mary was deeply disturbed, and wondered what sort of greeting this could be.

[30] The Messenger said to her, "Do not be afraid, Mary, for you have found favour with God. [31] You will become pregnant, and bear a son, and you are to call him Jesus. [32] He will be a great one, and will be called 'Son of the Most High', and the Lord God will give him the throne of his father David; [33] and he will rule over the house of Jacob forever, and his kingdom will never end."

[34] Mary said to the Messenger, "How can this be, since I am a virgin?"

[35] The Messenger replied, "The Holy Spirit will come upon you, and the power of the Most High will overshadow you. Therefore the child to be born will be holy, and will be called the Son of God. [36] Look, your cousin Elizabeth has even conceived a son in her old age, and this is the sixth month–she who was supposedly barren. [37] So nothing is impossible for God."

[38] Mary said, "I am the Lord's servant. May it all happen to me just as you say."

And the Messenger left her.

[39] Soon after, Mary got ready and went with some haste to the hill country, to a city in Judah. [40] She entered Zechariah's home, and called out a greeting to Elizabeth.

[41] When Elizabeth heard Mary's greeting, the baby kicked in her womb, and Elizabeth was filled with the Holy Spirit. [42] And she declared in a loud voice, "You are the most blessed of women, and blessed is the fruit of your womb! [43] And who am I that the mother of my Lord should visit me? [44] For as the sound of your greeting reached my ears, the baby within my womb kicked with joy. [45] Blessed is she who believed that what the Lord said to her would take place."

[46] And Mary said:

"My soul greatly honours the Lord,

[47] And my spirit rejoices because of God my Saviour,

[48] for he has taken notice of the humble state of his servant.

For from now on, every generation will call me blessed

[49] because the Mighty One has done great things for me–

His name is holy,

[50] And to generation after generation of people, he shows mercy to those who fear him.

[51] He has shown the strength of his arm, and scattered those who are arrogant in their hearts;

[52] he has knocked down rulers from their thrones; and he has lifted up the humble.

[53] He has filled the hungry with good things; but the rich he has sent away empty-handed.

[54] He has taken care of Israel, his son, remembering to be merciful,

[55] just as he promised to our fathers, to Abraham and his descendants for ever."

[56] Mary remained with her for about three months, and then returned home.

[57] Now the time finally came for Elizabeth to have her baby, and she gave birth to a son. [58] Her neighbours and relatives heard that the Lord had shown her such mercy, and they rejoiced with her.

[59] On the eighth day, they came to have the boy circumcised, and they were going to name him after his father, Zechariah. [60] But his mother said, "No, he is to be called John".

[61] They said to her, "No-one from your family has that name". [62] And they communicated with his father by signs, to see what he wanted to call him.

[63] Zechariah asked for something to write on, and wrote, "His name is John". And they were all amazed.

[64] Immediately, Zechariah's mouth was opened, and his tongue set free, and he began to praise God.

[65] And those who lived nearby were filled with awe, and in the mountain region of Judea

there was much discussion about all these events. [66] Everyone who heard about it could not help wondering, "What then will this child turn out to be?" For the hand of the Lord was with him.

[67] And his father Zechariah was filled with the Holy Spirit and prophesied:

[68] "Blessed be the Lord God of Israel, because he has come to us, and redeemed his people;
[69] he has raised up a mighty Saviour[†] for us in the family line of his servant, David,
[70] just as he promised through his holy prophets of old—
[71] rescue[††] from our enemies and from the hand of all who hate us,
[72] to show mercy to our fathers and to remember his holy covenant,
[73] an oath which he swore to our father Abraham—to grant us
[74] deliverance from the hand of our enemies, and to serve him without fear
[75] in holiness and righteousness in his presence all our days.
[76] And you, my son, will be called a prophet of the Most High;
for you will prophesy in advance of the Lord, to prepare his way,
[77] to make rescue known to his people by the forgiveness of their sins,
[78] through the compassionate mercy of our God, which will break on us like a sunrise from on high,
[79] to give light to those who sit in darkness and the shadow of death,
in order to guide our feet into the way of peace."

[80] The boy grew and became strong in spirit; and he lived in the desert until the time when he appeared publicly to Israel.

Chapter 2

[1] Around that time, a decree went out from Caesar Augustus to conduct a census of the known world—[2] this was the first census that took place when Quirinius was governor of Syria. [3] So everyone travelled back to their home towns to register, [4] including Joseph. He went up from Nazareth in Galilee to the city of David (which is called Bethlehem) in Judea, because he was from David's family line. [5] He took Mary with him to be registered, and she was pregnant.

[6] As it happened, while they were there in Bethlehem, the time came for her to have the baby, [7] and she gave birth to her firstborn son. And because there was no room for them in the inn, she used strips of cloth to wrap him up, and a food trough for his cradle.

[8] In that part of the country, there were shepherds who stayed out in the fields at night to keep watch over their flock. [9] Without warning, one of the Lord's angelic Messengers appeared to them, and the brilliance[†] of the Lord shone all around them. They were terrified, [10] but the Messenger said to them, "Do not be afraid. Listen, I am here to bring you news of great joy which is for all the people: [11] today, a Saviour has been born to you in the city of David. He is the Lord Christ. [12] And this will be the sign for you—you will find a child wrapped up in strips of cloth and lying in a food trough."[††]

[13] Suddenly, there appeared with the Messenger a vast company of the heavenly armies, praising God and saying, [14] "Glory to God in the highest, and peace on earth to those with whom he is pleased".

[15] After the angels had left them and gone back to heaven, the shepherds said to one another, "Come on, let's go into Bethlehem and see this thing which has taken place, which the Lord has

---

† Or *Rescuer*, also below.
†† Or *salvation*.

† Or *glory*.
†† Traditionally, *manger;* also below.

made known to us". ¹⁶ They went quickly, and discovered Mary and Joseph—and the baby lying in a food trough. ¹⁷ When they saw this, they revealed the message that had been told to them about this child, ¹⁸ and everyone who heard it was amazed at what the shepherds said. ¹⁹ Mary was taking note of these things, pondering them in her heart. ²⁰ The shepherds went back, glorifying and praising God for everything they had heard and seen, which had happened just as they had been told.

Jesus' Childhood

²¹ After eight days, the time came for him to be circumcised, and he was called Jesus, which was what the Messenger said to call him before he was conceived in the womb. ²² And when the days of their purification were over (according to the law of Moses), Joseph and Mary took him up to Jerusalem to present him to the Lord, ²³ just as it is written in the Law of the Lord, "Every firstborn male shall be holy to the Lord". ²⁴ They also went in order to offer a sacrifice, as the Law of the Lord says: a pair of turtledoves or two young pigeons.

²⁵ Now there was a man in Jerusalem named Simeon. He was a righteous and devout man, who was waiting for Israel to be comforted; and the Holy Spirit was upon him. ²⁶ It had been revealed to him by the Holy Spirit that he would not see death before he had seen the Lord's Christ.

²⁷ Through the influence of the Spirit, he went into the temple. And when the parents of the boy Jesus came in, to do what the custom of the law required concerning him, ²⁸ Simeon took him in his arms and blessed God, and said,

²⁹ "Now, Master, you may let your servant depart in peace, as you promised,

³⁰ because with my own eyes I have seen your salvation[†]

³¹ which you have prepared for all peoples to see—

³² a revealing light for the other nations, and so your people Israel will be glorified."

³³ His father and mother were amazed at what was said about him, ³⁴ and Simeon blessed them and said to Mary, his mother, "This one is destined to cause the falling and rising of many in Israel, and to be a sign that is spoken against— ³⁵ and as for you, a sword will pierce your own soul—and thus the thoughts of many hearts will be revealed".

³⁶ In the temple there was also a prophetess called Anna, the daughter of Phanuel, from the tribe of Asher. She was very old, having lived with her husband seven years after her marriage, ³⁷ and then as a widow for eighty-four years. She never left the temple, worshipping God with fasting and prayers night and day. ³⁸ She came up to them at that very moment, and gave thanks to God, and began to speak about the child to all those who were waiting for the redemption of Jerusalem.

³⁹ When they had finished all that the Law of the Lord required, Joseph and Mary returned to their own city of Nazareth in Galilee. ⁴⁰ The boy grew and became strong, and full of wisdom. And the grace of God was with him.

⁴¹ Each year his parents went to Jerusalem for the Feast of the Passover[†], ⁴² and when he was twelve they went up for the Feast according to the custom.

⁴³ When the days of the Feast were completed, they began their return journey, but the boy Jesus remained behind in Jerusalem without his parents knowing. ⁴⁴ They thought that he was somewhere in their group, and they had gone a day's journey before they started to look for him among their relatives and friends. ⁴⁵ Finding nothing, they returned to Jerusalem to search for him. ⁴⁶ After three days, they found him in the temple, sitting among the teachers, listening to them and asking questions. ⁴⁷ All those who

†   An annual festival celebrating the Exodus of the Israelites from Egypt.

†   Or *rescue*.

heard him were astonished at his level of under-standing, and his answers.

[48] When they saw him there, his parents were very surprised and his mother said to him, "Son, why did you treat us like this? Look, your father and I have been very worried searching for you."

[49] He said to them, "Why did you have to search for me? Didn't you realise that I must be in my father's house?" [50] But they didn't understand what he was saying to them.

[51] So Jesus went back with his parents to Nazareth, and was obedient to them. And his mother treasured all these things in her heart. [52] Jesus grew in wisdom and stature, and in the favour of God and those who knew him.

Chapter 3

Preparations for Jesus' Public Career

[1] It was the fifteenth year of the reign of Tiberius Caesar. Pontius Pilate was governor of Judea, Herod was tetrarch of Galilee, his brother Phillip tetrarch of Iturea and Traconitis, and Lysanias was tetrarch of Abilene. [2] It was at this time, during the high priesthood of Annas and Caiaphas, that the word of God came to John, the son of Zechariah, in the desert.

[3] He went throughout the country around the Jordan, proclaiming a baptism† of repentance†† for the forgiveness of sins. [4] As it is written in the scroll of the words of Isaiah the prophet:

"A voice crying out in the desert:
'Prepare the way of the Lord;
make his paths straight;
[5] every valley will be filled in,
and every mountain and hill will be levelled;
the crooked roads will become straight,

and the rough tracks smooth.
[6] And all humanity will see the salvation†
of God.'"

[7] So John said to the crowds that had come out to be baptized by him, "You snakes! Who warned you to flee from the coming Anger?†† [8] Therefore, produce fruits that are worthy of repentance. And do not start to say to yourselves, 'We have Abraham as our father'. For I tell you that God is able to raise up children of Abraham from these rocks. [9] Indeed, the axe is already poised at the root of the trees; and every tree that does not produce good fruit is cut down and thrown into the fire."

[10] "What should we do then?" the crowds asked him.

[11] He answered them, "The one who has two shirts should donate one to someone who has none; and the one who has food should do the same".

[12] Tax collectors* also came to be baptized by him, and said to him, "Teacher, what should we do?"

[13] And John answered them, "Take no more than you are supposed to collect".

[14] Soldiers also asked him, "What about us; what should we do?"

And he said to them, "Don't threaten people for money, or be corrupt, but be content with your wages".

[15] The expectations of the people began to rise, and everyone wondered in their hearts whether he might not be the Christ.

[16] In answer to this, John said to all of them, "I baptize you with water; but someone much stronger than me is coming—I would not even be worthy to undo the strap of his sandal. He will

---

† An initiation rite common among Jews of the period.
†† Literally, 'a change of outlook or mind', used here of returning to God.

† i.e. *rescue.*
†† Or *wrath.*
* That is, Jews who collaborated with the occupying Roman forces to collect taxes from their fellow Jews. They were widely hated, and excluded from Jewish religious life.

baptize you with the Holy Spirit and fire. [17] He has the winnowing fork in his hand to clean out his threshing floor, and gather the grain into his barn. But he will burn up the chaff with unquenchable fire."

[18] Thus, with many other warnings, John announced the news to the people.

[19] But when John rebuked Herod the tetrarch for taking Herodias, his brother's wife, and for all the other wicked things he had done, [20] Herod added this to them all: he locked up John in prison.

[21] Now when all the people had been baptized, and Jesus also had been baptized and was praying, heaven was opened, [22] and the Holy Spirit came down upon him in the form of a dove. And a voice came from heaven, "You are my beloved son; with you I am very pleased".

[23] Jesus himself was about thirty when it all really began. He was the son (so it was thought) of Joseph:

who was the son of Heli,
[24] the son of Matthat,
the son of Levi,
the son of Melchi,
the son of Jannai,
the son of Joseph,
[25] the son of Mattathias,
the son of Amos,
the son of Nahum,
the son of Esli,
the son of Naggai,
[26] the son of Maath,
the son of Mattathias,
the son of Semein,
the son of Josech,
the son of Joda,
[27] the son of Jo-anan,
the son of Rhesa,
the son of Zerubbabel,
the son of Shealtiel,
the son of Neri,

[28] the son of Melchi,
the son of Addi,
the son of Cosam,
the son of Elmadam,
the son of Er,
[29] the son of Joshua,
the son of Eliezer,
the son of Jorim,
the son of Matthat,
the son of Levi,
[30] the son of Simeon,
the son of Judah,
the son of Joseph,
the son of Jonam,
the son of Eliakim,
[31] the son of Melea,
the son of Menna,
the son of Mattatha,
the son of Nathan,
the son of David,
[32] the son of Jesse,
the son of Obed,
the son of Boaz,
the son of Sala,
the son of Nahshon,
[33] the son of Amminadab,
the son of Admin,
the son of Arni,
the son of Hezron,
the son of Perez,
the son of Judah,
[34] the son of Jacob,
the son of Isaac,
the son of Abraham,
the son of Terah,
the son of Nahor,
[35] the son of Serug,
the son of Reu,
the son of Peleg,
the son of Eber,
the son of Shelah,
[36] the son of Cainan,
the son of Arphaxad,

the son of Shem,
the son of Noah,
the son of Lamech,
[37] the son of Methuselah,
the son of Enoch,
the son of Jared,
the son of Mahalaleel,
the son of Cainan,
[38] the son of Enosh,
the son of Seth,
the son of Adam,
the son of God.

Chapter 4

[1] Full of the Holy Spirit, Jesus returned from the Jordan and was brought by the Spirit into the desert [2] for forty days, where he was tested by the devil.

During that time he ate nothing, and by the end of it he was hungry. [3] So the devil said to him, "If you are the son of God, tell this rock to become bread".

[4] But Jesus answered him, "It is written in the Scriptures, 'Man will not live by bread alone'".

[5] Then the devil led him up high and showed him all the kingdoms of the world in a moment of time. [6] And the devil said to him, "I will give all this authority to you, and the glory of all these kingdoms, because it is mine to give. And I can give it to anyone I wish. [7] If, then, you will worship me, all of it will be yours."

[8] But Jesus replied, "It is written, 'You are to worship the Lord your God, and serve him alone'".

[9] Then he took him to Jerusalem, stood him on the pinnacle of the temple and said to him, "If you are the son of God, throw yourself down from here, [10] for it is written, 'He will command his angels concerning you, to keep watch over you', [11] and 'They will bear you up on their hands, in case you should strike your foot against a rock'".

[12] Jesus answered him, "It is said, 'Do not put the Lord your God to the test'".

[13] And when the devil had finished every test, he left Jesus until an opportune time.

Jesus Begins his Public Career in Galilee[†]

[14] Jesus returned in the power of the Spirit to Galilee, and a report about him spread throughout the whole region. [15] He taught in their synagogues, and everybody spoke glowingly of him.

[16] He came to Nazareth where he had grown up, and according to his custom, he went into the synagogue on the Sabbath[††] day. He stood up to read, [17] and the scroll of the prophet Isaiah was handed to him. Unrolling it, he found the place where it was written, [18] "The Spirit of the Lord is upon me, because he has anointed me to announce great news to the poor; he has sent me to proclaim release for prisoners, and sight once more for the blind, to send the oppressed away free; [19] to proclaim the acceptable year of the Lord".

[20] Rolling up the scroll, he gave it to the assistant and sat down. And the eyes of everyone in the synagogue were fixed on him.

[21] He began to speak to them, "Today, this Scripture is fulfilled in your hearing".

[22] And they were all speaking about him, and were amazed at the gracious words which came out of his mouth. They said, "Isn't this Joseph's son?"

[23] And he said to them, "No doubt you will quote this proverb to me, 'Physician, heal yourself! What we have heard you did in Capernaum, do here as well in your home town.'"

[24] But he went on, "Truly, I tell you that no prophet is acceptable in his home town. [25] Truly, I tell you, there were many widows in Elijah's time in Israel, when the heavens were shut for three years and six months, and a great famine settled on the whole land. [26] Elijah was sent to

---

†   That is, the northern part of Israel.
†† That is, from sunset Friday to sunset Saturday, the day of rest set down in the Law of Moses.

none of them, but to the widow of Zarephath in Sidon. [27] And there were many lepers in Israel in the time of Elisha the prophet, but none of them were cleansed; only Naaman the Syrian."

[28] When they heard this in the synagogue, they were all filled with rage. [29] Rising up, they ran him out of the city, and led him to the edge of the cliff on which their city was built, in order to throw him down. [30] But he passed straight through their midst, and went on his way.

[31] Then he went down to Capernaum, which was a city in Galilee, and he was teaching them on the Sabbath Day. [32] They were astonished at his teaching, because he spoke with authority.

[33] Now in the synagogue there was a man with an unclean demonic spirit, and he called out in a loud voice, [34] "Hey! What have you to do with us, Jesus of Nazareth? Have you come to destroy us? I know who you are: the holy one of God!"

[35] Jesus rebuked him, and said, "Be silent, and come out of him". And after hurling the man down in their midst, the demon came out of him. The man was unharmed.

[36] They were all awe-struck, and said to one another, "What sort of word is this, that commands the unclean spirits with authority and power, and they come out?"

[37] And reports about him spread throughout the region.

[38] Jesus stood up and left the synagogue, and went to Simon's house. Simon's mother-in-law was in the grip of a high fever, and they asked him to do something for her.

[39] Jesus stood over her and rebuked the fever, and it left her. She got straight up and began to serve them.

[40] As the sun was setting, everyone who had any who were sick with various diseases brought them to him. He laid his hands on each one of them, and healed them. [41] And demons were coming out of many people, calling out, "You are the son of God!" Yet Jesus rebuked them, and would not allow them to speak, because they knew that he was the Christ.

[42] When it was day, he went out into a place in the desert, and the crowds were looking for him. [43] But he said to them, "I must announce the good news of the kingdom of God to the other cities as well, because that is why I was sent".

[44] And he went on preaching in the synagogues of Galilee.

Chapter 5

[1] On one occasion, he was standing by Lake Gennesaret and the crowd was pressing in on him to hear the message of God. [2] He saw two boats on the edge of the lake, left there by the fishermen who were cleaning the nets. [3] He got into one of the boats, which belonged to Simon, and asked him to put out a little way from the land. When he had sat down, he taught the crowd from the boat.

[4] When he had finished speaking, he said to Simon, "Put out into the deeper water, and let down your nets for a catch".

[5] Simon answered, "Master, we have been working hard all night without getting a thing. But if you say so, I will let down the nets."

[6] Having done so, they netted a huge quantity of fish, and their nets began to tear. [7] They waved to their partners in the other boat to come and help them, and they came and filled both boats to the point of sinking.

[8] Seeing all this, Simon Peter[†] fell at Jesus' knees and said, "Go away from me, Lord, for I am a sinful man". [9] For he was gripped with fear and amazement (as were all those with him) at the catch of fish they had taken. [10] James and John, the sons of Zebedee, who were Simon's partners, felt the same. And Jesus said to Simon, "Don't be afraid. From now on, you will catch people."

[11] And after they had brought the boats to

---

† Jesus later gave Simon the additional name 'Peter'.

shore, they left everything, and followed him.

[12] In one of the cities Jesus was visiting, there was a man covered with leprosy. When he saw Jesus, he fell down before him and begged him, "Lord, if you are willing, you can make me clean".

[13] Jesus stretched out his hand and touched him, and said, "I am willing. Be clean." And immediately the leprosy disappeared. [14] Jesus commanded the man not to say anything. "Instead, go and show yourself to the priest, and bring the offerings for your purification, as Moses commanded. This will be a testimony to them."

[15] But reports about him spread all the more, and a great crowd gathered to hear him and to be healed from their sicknesses.

[16] But he used to withdraw into the desert and pray.

[17] One day, Jesus was teaching, and some Pharisees[†] and teachers of the Law[††] were sitting there. They had come from all the towns of Galilee and Judea and Jerusalem. And the power of the Lord was with him to heal.

[18] Some men arrived carrying a paralysed man on a stretcher. They were trying to bring him in to put him before Jesus, [19] but because of the crowd, they could find no way through. They went up onto the roof of the house, and lowered him down on his stretcher through the tiles, right into their midst in front of Jesus. [20] When Jesus saw their faith, he said, "Friend, your sins are forgiven".

[21] The Scribes and Pharisees began to think to themselves, "Who is this who speaks such blasphemies? Who is able to forgive sins except God alone?"

[22] But Jesus realised what they were thinking, and answered them, "Why do you think this way in your hearts? [23] Which is easier: to say, 'Your sins are forgiven' or to say, 'Get up and walk'? [24] But so that you may know that the Son of Man[†] has authority on earth to forgive sins...". He said to the paralysed man, "I tell you, get up, and pick up your stretcher and go back home".

[25] And immediately he got up right there in front of them, picked up what he was lying on and went back to his home, giving honour and praise to God.

[26] Everybody was stunned, and honoured God. They were quite afraid, and said, "We have seen extraordinary things today".

[27] After this, Jesus went out and saw a tax collector named Levi sitting at the tax collecting booth. He said to him, "Follow me", [28] and he got up, left everything, and followed him. [29] And Levi held a great feast for Jesus at his house, with a large crowd of tax collectors; and others were there as well, reclining at the table with them.[††]

[30] Now the Pharisees and Scribes complained to his disciples, "Why do you eat and drink with tax collectors and sinners?"

[31] And Jesus replied, "It is not the healthy who need a doctor, but the sick. [32] I have not come to invite the righteous, but sinners to repentance."

[33] They said to him, "John's disciples are always fasting and praying, and so are the disciples of the Pharisees. But yours eat and drink!"

[34] Jesus replied, "Are you able to make wedding guests fast while the bridegroom is with them? [35] But the days will come when the bridegroom is taken away from them, and then they will fast."

[36] He also told them this parable*: "No-one tears a piece off a new garment and sews it onto an old one—you would not only ruin the new

---

† 'Son of Man' was a common Jewish way of referring to oneself in the third person (as 'oneself' is in English). Jesus also used this expression to refer back to an exalted figure in Old Testament prophecy, the 'Son of Man' of Daniel 7.

†† People did not sit on chairs to eat in the ancient world; they had low tables, and reclined on cushions or couches to eat.

* A short proverbial saying or story.

---

† A strict religious group among the Jews.

†† Also described in Luke as 'Scribes' and 'religious lawyers'.

one, but the piece from the new would not match the old. [37] And no-one pours young wine into old wineskins–the young wine would burst the wineskins, the wine would spill everywhere, and the wineskins would be ruined. [38] No, young wine must go into new wineskins. [39] And no-one, having drunk old wine, prefers young wine; for he says, 'The old is good'."

Chapter 6

[1] Now it happened that he was walking through the grainfields on a Sabbath Day, and his disciples were plucking the heads of grain, rubbing them in their hands, and eating them. [2] Some of the Pharisees said, "Why are you doing what is unlawful on the Sabbath?"

[3] Jesus answered them by saying, "Haven't you read what David did when he and his men were hungry? [4] He went into the house of God, took the special bread for the offering, and ate it; and he gave some to those who were with him. And this was the bread that was unlawful to eat, except for the priests alone." [5] He said to them, "The Son of Man is Lord of the Sabbath".

[6] On another Sabbath Day, he went into the synagogue to teach. And a man was there with a deformed right hand. [7] The Scribes and Pharisees were watching Jesus in case he healed on the Sabbath, so that they could accuse him.

[8] But Jesus knew what they were thinking. He said to the man with the deformed hand, "Get up and stand here in the middle". And he rose and stood there.

[9] Jesus said to them, "Let me ask you, on the Sabbath is it lawful to do good or to do evil? To save life or destroy?" [10] Looking round at all of them, he said to the man, "Stretch out your hand". He did so, and his hand was restored.

[11] This made them furious, and they began to discuss with one another what they might do to Jesus.

[12] Around that time, he went out to the moun-tain to pray, and spent all night in prayer to God. [13] When it was day, he summoned his disciples, and chose twelve of them, whom he called apostles.[†] [14] There was Simon (also called Peter), Andrew his brother, James, John, Philip, Bartholomew, [15] Matthew, Thomas, James (son of Alphaeus), Simon (called the Zealot), [16] Judas (son of James) and Judas Iscariot, who became a traitor.

[17] He went down with them to a plain, along with a great crowd of his disciples. And a huge number of people from all over Judea and Jerusalem and the coastal region of Tyre and Sidon, [18] came to hear him and to be healed of their diseases. Those who were troubled by unclean spirits were also being healed. [19] The whole crowd was trying to touch him, because power was emanating from him and healing everyone.

[20] Then he turned his attention to his disciples, and said,

"Blessed are you poor, because the kingdom of God belongs to you.

[21] "Blessed are you who are hungry now, because you will be fed.

"Blessed are you who weep now, because you will laugh.

[22] "Blessed are you when people hate you and ostracise you and criticise you and blacken your name on account of the Son of Man. [23] Rejoice and leap for joy in that day, for great is your reward in heaven; for the fathers of those who persecute you used to do the same to the prophets.

[24] "However, woe to you who are rich, because you are receiving your comfort.

[25] "Woe to you who are full now, because you will be hungry.

"Woe to you who laugh now, because you will mourn and weep.

[26] "Woe to you when everyone speaks well of

† 'Apostle' literally means 'one sent out (for a task)'. In the New Testament, it usually refers to those sent out to continue Jesus' preaching.

you, for their fathers used to do the same to the false prophets.

[27] "But to you who are listening, I say: Love your enemies. Do good to those who hate you. [28] Bless those who curse you. Pray for those who mistreat you. [29] If someone strikes you on the cheek, offer him the other cheek as well; and if someone takes your coat, let him have your shirt as well. [30] To everyone who asks of you, give; and if someone takes your things, don't demand them back. [31] And in the way you want people to treat you, do the same for them.

[32] "If you love those who love you, what credit is that to you? For even the sinners love those who love them. [33] And if you do good to those who do good to you, what credit is that to you? Even the sinners do that. [34] And if you lend to those you know will return the favour, what credit is that to you? Even sinners lend to sinners so that they might receive as much back.

[35] "But love your enemies, and do good and lend without expecting anything. Your reward will be great, and you will be sons of the Most High[†], because he shows kindness to the ungrateful and the wicked. [36] Be merciful, as your Father is merciful. [37] And do not judge, or else you also will be judged. Do not condemn, or else you also will be condemned. Forgive, and you will be forgiven. [38] Give, and it will be given to you—a good amount, pressed down, shaken and running over, will be put in your lap—for the amount you give will be the amount you get back."

[39] He also told them a parable: "Can the blind lead the blind? Will they not both fall into a ditch? [40] The student[††] is not above the teacher; but everyone who has been fully trained will be like his teacher.

[41] "Why do you notice the speck that is in your brother's eye, but do not consider the log that is in your own? [42] How can you possibly say to your brother, 'Brother, let me take the speck out of your eye', when you haven't noticed the log in your own eye. You hypocrite! First take the log out of your own eye, and then you will be able to see clearly to remove the speck from your brother's eye.

[43] "For a good tree never produces rotten fruit; nor does a rotten tree produce good fruit, [44] because each tree is known by its own fruit. Figs are not gathered from thorn bushes, nor are grapes picked from bramble bushes. [45] A good man brings out good things from the good treasure of his heart; and an evil man brings forth evil from the evil in his heart. For his mouth speaks from the overflow of the heart.

[46] "Why do you call me 'Lord, Lord', but do not do what I say? [47] Everyone who comes to me and hears my message and puts it into practice— let me show you what that person is like: [48] He is like a man who was building a house, and who dug down deep and laid the foundation on solid rock. When a flood came, the river burst upon that house, but could not shake it, because the house was well built. [49] However, the person who hears but does not put into practice is like a man who built a house on the soil, without a foundation. And when the river burst upon it, the house collapsed immediately, and was utterly ruined."

Chapter 7

[1] After Jesus had completed all his teachings in the hearing of the people, he entered Capernaum. [2] Now a certain centurion had a highly-valued servant, who was ill to the point of death. [3] When the centurion heard about Jesus, he sent some Jewish elders to ask him whether he could come, so that the servant might escape death.

[4] They came to Jesus and strongly urged him, "This man is worthy of your help, [5] for he loves our people and even built our synagogue".

[6] So Jesus went with them. When he was not

---

† To be sons of was a Jewish way of saying you were like someone or something; that you 'bore the family likeness'.

†† Literally, disciple.

far from the house, the centurion sent friends to say to him, "Lord, do not trouble yourself, for I do not deserve to have you come under my roof. [7] And neither did I count myself worthy to come to see you. But say the word and my servant will be healed. [8] For I too am a man under authority, and I have soldiers under me. I say to this one, 'Go' and he goes, and to another 'Come here' and he comes, and to my servant, 'Do this', and he does it."

[9] When he heard this, Jesus was amazed at him, and turning to the crowd that was following him, said, "I tell you, not even in Israel have I found faith such as this!"

[10] And those who had been sent to Jesus returned to the house, and found the servant well again.

[11] Not long afterwards, Jesus went to a city called Nain, and his disciples and a great crowd went with him. [12] As he drew near the gate of the city, he saw that they were carrying out a dead person, who was the only son of his widowed mother. A crowd from the city was with the widow. [13] When he saw her, the Lord had compassion for her, and said, "Don't cry". [14] And he stepped forward and laid his hand on the coffin. The pall-bearers stood still, and he said, "Young man, I say to you, rise up!"

[15] The dead man sat up and began to speak, and Jesus gave him to his mother.

[16] Fear took hold of everyone, and they glorified God, saying, "A great prophet has arisen amongst us" and "God has visited his people". [17] And this report about him spread through all of Judea and the surrounding region.

[18] John's disciples told him about all these things. So John selected two of his disciples, [19] and sent them to the Lord to ask, "Are you the Coming One, or should we wait for another?" [20] The men came to Jesus and said, "John the Baptist sent us to you to ask, 'Are you the Coming One or should we wait for another?'"

[21] At that particular time, Jesus healed many people from illnesses and diseases and evil spirits, and he gave many blind people back their sight. [22] He answered the men, "Go back and tell John what you see and hear: the blind see, the crippled walk, and the lepers are being cleansed; the deaf hear, the dead are being raised, and the poor are hearing the great news. [23] And blessed is the one who does not stumble because of me."

[24] When John's messengers had departed, he began to talk to the crowd about John: "What did you go out into the desert to see? A reed being shaken by the wind? [25] What did you go out to see? A man dressed in fancy clothes? No, those who have gorgeous clothes and luxuries live in royal palaces. [26] So what did you go out to see? A prophet? Yes, I tell you, and much more than a prophet. [27] He is the one about whom it is written in the Scriptures, 'See, I send my messenger before your face, who will prepare the way before you'. [28] I tell you, among those born of women, none is greater than John; but the person who is least in the kingdom of God is greater than John!"

[29] (And when all the people heard this, including the tax collectors, they considered God justified, since they had been baptized with John's baptism. [30] However, the Pharisees and religious lawyers, who had not been baptized by him, rejected God's purpose for themselves.)

[31] "To what, then, shall I compare the people of this generation? What are they like? [32] They are like children sitting in the marketplace, calling out to one another, 'We played the flute for you and you didn't dance; we wailed and you didn't weep'. [33] For John the Baptist came not eating bread nor drinking wine, and you say, 'He has a demon!' [34] The Son of Man came eating and drinking, and you say, 'Look, he's a glutton and a drunkard, a friend of tax collectors and sinners'. [35] Yet wisdom is considered justified by all her children."

[36] One of the Pharisees invited Jesus to dine with him, and Jesus went to the Pharisee's house, and reclined at the table. [37] Now there was a woman in the city who was a sinner, and when

she found out that Jesus was having dinner at the Pharisee's house, she brought an alabaster jar of perfumed lotion. [38] She stood behind Jesus, near his feet, crying; and her tears were wetting his feet, and she started to wipe his feet with her hair and to kiss them, and to anoint them with the lotion.

[39] When the Pharisee who invited Jesus saw this, he said to himself, "If this man were a prophet, he would realise who she was and what kind of woman was touching him—that she is a sinner".

[40] And Jesus answered him, "Simon, I have something to say to you".

"Teacher", he said, "go ahead and speak".

[41] "There were two people in debt to a certain money-lender. One owed him the equivalent of 500 day's wages; the other 50.[†] [42] Neither of them were able to pay, and so the money-lender forgave both debts. Which of them, then, will love him more?"

[43] Simon answered, "I suppose the one who was forgiven more".

He said to him, "You have judged rightly".

[44] And turning to the woman, he said to Simon, "Do you see this woman? I came into your house—you did not provide water for my feet; but she has been wetting my feet with her tears and wiping them with her hair. [45] You gave me no kiss; but from the time I arrived she has not stopped kissing my feet. [46] You did not anoint my head with oil; but she has anointed my feet with lotion. [47] And so I say to you, she has had many sins forgiven; thus, she loves much. But he who is forgiven little, loves little."

[48] He said to her, "Your sins are forgiven".

[49] And those who were reclining at the table with him, began to say to themselves, "Who is this, who even forgives sins?"

[50] He said to the woman, "Your faith has rescued you; go in peace".

---

† Literally 500 denarii and 50 denarii. The denarius was a day's wage for a labourer.

Chapter 8

[1] Soon after this, Jesus travelled through the cities and towns, preaching and announcing the great news of the kingdom of God, and the twelve apostles were with him. [2] Certain women who had been healed of evil spirits and illnesses were also with him—Mary who was called Magdalene (from whom seven demons had been cast out), [3] Joanna (the wife of Herod's steward Chuza), Susanna, and many others. These women provided for them out of their own money.

[4] A great crowd was gathering, coming to him from every city. So he told a parable:

[5] "A sower went out to sow his seed. And while he was sowing, some of the seed fell on the path and was trampled on, and the birds ate it. [6] Other seed fell on rocky ground, and as soon as it grew it withered, because it had no moisture. [7] Still other seed fell in the midst of thorns, and the thorns grew up alongside, and choked it. [8] But other seed fell in good soil, and having grown, it produced a massive crop." After saying this, he called out, "Let anyone with ears to hear, listen!"

[9] His disciples asked him what this parable meant. [10] He said to them, "You have been granted to know the secret of the kingdom of God, but for the rest it is all in parables, so that even though they 'see' they may not see, and even though they hear they may not understand. [11] This is what the parable means: The seed is the message of God. [12] The seed which fell on the path represents those who hear, but then the devil comes and takes the message from their heart, so that they may not believe and be rescued. [13] The seed which fell on the rocky ground stands for those who, when they hear, receive the message with joy. But they do not have any root. They believe for a while, but when the time of testing comes, they pull back.

[14] "Now the seed which fell into the thorns represents those who hear, but as they go along, they are choked by the worries and riches and pleasures of life; and they never mature to produce fruit. [15] And the seed which fell in good

soil—these are the people who hear the message, and hold onto it in their good and noble hearts, and, in persevering, produce fruit.

16 "No-one after lighting a lamp covers it with a bowl or puts it under the bed, but places it on a lampstand, so that those who come in might see the light. 17 For there is nothing hidden that will not become plain, and nothing concealed that will not become known and come to light. 18 Be careful, then, how you listen. For whoever has, more will be given to him; but whoever does not have, even what he seems to have will be taken away from him."

19 Jesus' mother and brothers arrived to see him, but they were not able to reach him because of the crowd. 20 And someone told him, "Your mother and brothers are standing outside, wanting to see you". 21 Jesus replied, "These are my mother and brothers—those who hear the message of God and put it into practice".

22 One day, he got into a boat with his disciples and said to them, "Let us go across to the other side of the lake". They set out, 23 and while they were sailing, he fell asleep. Then a windstorm came down the lake. The boat was filling with water and they were in real danger.

24 They went and woke Jesus and said, "Master, Master, we are about to die!" But he got up and rebuked the wind and the raging water, and they stopped, and it became calm.

25 He said to the disciples, "Where is your faith?" They were afraid and astonished, and said to one another, "Who then is this, that he commands even the winds and the water, and they obey him?"

26 They sailed on to the country of the Gerasenes, which is on the shore opposite Galilee. 27 When he got out of the boat, he was met by a certain man from the city, who had demons. For a long time he had not worn clothes, and he lived among the tombs rather than in a house.

28 When he saw Jesus, he cried out and fell down before him, and said in a loud voice, "What have I got to do with you, Jesus, son of the Most High God? I beg you, do not torment me." 29 For Jesus had commanded the unclean spirit to come out of the man. Many times it had seized him, and he used to be bound with chains and shackles, and kept under guard. But he would break the bonds, and be driven by the demon into the desert.

30 Jesus asked him, "What is your name?" And he replied, "Legion", because many demons had gone into him. 31 And they pleaded with him not to order them to depart into the abyss.

32 Now there was a good-sized herd of pigs grazing on the hillside; and the demons begged him to permit them to enter the pigs, and he allowed them to do so. 33 The demons left the man and went into the pigs, and the herd rushed over the cliff into the lake and was drowned.

34 When those who were looking after the pigs saw this, they fled, and reported it to those in the city and in the country, who then came out to see what had happened. 35 They came to Jesus and found the man from whom the demons had been driven out sitting at Jesus' feet, clothed and in his right mind. And they were afraid. 36 Those who had seen it all, explained how the demon-possessed man had been rescued.[†]

37 Then all those from the region of the Gerasenes asked him to go away from them, for they were gripped with great fear. And getting back into the boat, he returned.

38 The man from whom the demons had come out begged to go with him, but Jesus sent him away, saying, 39 "Go back to your home, and tell what God has done for you". And he went through the whole city, declaring what Jesus had done for him.

40 When Jesus returned, a crowd was there to welcome him, for they had all been waiting for him. 41 A man named Jairus, who was a ruler of the synagogue, came straight up to Jesus and fell

† Or *saved,* or *healed,* also below.

at his feet, and begged him to come to his house. [42] The reason was that his only daughter, who was about twelve years old, was dying.

While Jesus was on his way, the crowds almost crushed him. [43] Among them was a woman who had suffered from a flow of blood for twelve years, and no-one had been able to cure her, though she had spent all her resources on doctors. [44] Coming up behind Jesus, she touched the fringe of his clothes, and immediately the flow of blood ceased.

[45] Jesus said, "Who touched me?" They all denied it, and Peter said, "Master, the crowds are pressing in and crushing you".

[46] But Jesus said, "Someone touched me, for I know that power has gone out from me".

[47] When the woman saw that she could not hide, she came trembling and fell down before him. And she declared before everyone why she had touched him, and how she had been instantly healed.

[48] He said to her, "Daughter, your faith has rescued you. Go in peace."

[49] While he was still speaking, someone came from the synagogue ruler's house and said to Jairus, "Your daughter is dead. Do not trouble the teacher any longer."

[50] Jesus heard this, and said to him, "Don't be afraid; only have faith and she will be rescued".

[51] When he came to the house, he let no-one go in with him except Peter, James and John, and the girl's father and mother. [52] Everyone was weeping and mourning for her, but he said, "Do not weep. For she is not dead, only sleeping." [53] And they laughed at him, because they knew she had died.

[54] Jesus grasped her hand, and called out, "Child, rise up!"

[55] And her spirit returned and she sat up immediately; and he ordered that she be given something to eat.

[56] Her parents were astounded, and he commanded them not to say what had happened.

Chapter 9

[1] He called together the twelve, and gave them power and authority over all the demons, and to heal sicknesses. [2] And he sent them out to proclaim the kingdom of God and to heal the sick. [3] He said to them, "Take nothing for the journey— no staff, no bag, no bread, no money, not even a spare shirt. [4] And whatever house you enter, stay there, and leave from there. [5] Wherever they do not welcome you, shake the dust off your feet as you leave that city, as a testimony to them."

[6] They set out, and went through the towns announcing the great news and healing everywhere.

[7] Now Herod the tetrarch heard about all these happenings. He was perplexed, because it was being said by some that John had been raised from the dead, [8] and by others that Elijah had appeared; and others were saying that an ancient prophet had risen up.

[9] Herod said, "John I beheaded; but who is this man I am hearing these things about?" And he tried to see him.

[10] When the apostles returned, they reported to Jesus what they had done. And taking them with him, he withdrew privately to a city called Bethsaida.

[11] But the crowds found out, and followed him. He welcomed them, and spoke to them about the kingdom of God, and cured those who were in need of healing. [12] The day was drawing to a close, and the twelve came and said to him, "Send the crowd away, so that they can go into the surrounding towns and fields to lodge, and to find food—for this place is a desert".

[13] But Jesus said to them, "Give them something to eat yourselves". They said, "We don't have more than five loaves of bread and two fish; unless perhaps we should go and buy provisions for all these people!" [14] (for there were about 5000 men).

He said to his disciples, "Sit them down in groups of 50". [15] And they did so, and the crowd all sat down.

¹⁶ Taking the five loaves and two fish, Jesus looked up to heaven, blessed them, broke them, and kept giving them to the disciples to set before the crowd.

¹⁷ And they ate and were all satisfied. The leftovers were gathered up, and there were twelve baskets of pieces.

¹⁸ Once, while he was praying alone, with his disciples close by, he asked them a question: "Who do the crowds say that I am?"

¹⁹ And they answered, "John the Baptist; others say Elijah, and others that an ancient prophet has risen up".

²⁰ He said to them, "And you, who do you say I am?"

Peter answered, "The Christ of God".

²¹ And he sternly commanded them not to say this to anyone, ²² saying, "The Son of Man must suffer much, and be rejected by the elders and Chief Priests and scribes, and be killed, and on the third day be raised up".

²³ He said to them all, "If anyone wants to come after me, let him deny himself and pick up his cross each day, and follow me. ²⁴ For whoever wants to save his life will lose it; but whoever loses his life for my sake—he will save it. ²⁵ For what profit does a person get if he gains the whole world, but loses or forfeits his very self? ²⁶ For whoever is ashamed of me and my words, the Son of Man will be ashamed of him when he comes in his glory and in the glory of the Father and the holy angels. ²⁷ I tell you the truth, there are some standing here who will not taste death until they see the kingdom of God."

²⁸ About eight days after he had said these things, Jesus took Peter, John and James up to the mountain to pray. ²⁹ As he was praying, the appearance of his face changed, and his clothing became white like lightning. ³⁰ Suddenly two men were there speaking with him—Moses and Elijah. ³¹ They appeared in brilliant glory, and spoke about his departure†, which he was about to complete in Jerusalem.

³² Now Peter and those with him were drowsy with sleep, but they woke up and saw his glory, and the two men who were standing with him. ³³ And when they were starting to separate from Jesus to leave, Peter said to him, "Master, it is good that we are here. Let us make three tents—one for you, and one for Moses, and one for Elijah". (He didn't know what he was saying.)

³⁴ While Peter was still saying this, a cloud came and surrounded them. They were afraid as they entered the cloud, ³⁵ and a voice came from out of the cloud and said, "This is my chosen Son; listen to him".

³⁶ And when the voice had spoken, Jesus was found alone. They kept quiet and told no-one at that time about anything that they had seen.

³⁷ The next day, after they had come down from the mountain, a great crowd was there to meet him. ³⁸ A man from the crowd cried out, "Teacher, I beg you to look at my son, because he is my only child. ³⁹ A spirit keeps on seizing him; it suddenly calls out and throws him into convulsions, with foaming at the mouth. It is destroying him, and hardly ever leaves him. ⁴⁰ I pleaded with your disciples to cast it out, but they were not able to."

⁴¹ Jesus answered, "O faithless and perverse generation, how long do I have to be with you and put up with you? Bring your son here."

⁴² While the boy was still coming forward, the demon attacked him and threw him into convulsions. But Jesus rebuked the unclean spirit and healed the boy, and returned him to his father.

⁴³ They were all amazed at the majesty of God. But while they were marvelling at all the things he was doing, he said to his disciples, ⁴⁴ "Let this sink in: the Son of Man is about to be betrayed into the hands of men". ⁴⁵ They didn't understand this; indeed, it was hidden from them so that they didn't perceive it. And they were afraid to ask him what he meant.

⁴⁶ Now a discussion arose among them as to which of them was the greatest. ⁴⁷ Knowing what

†   Literally, *his exodus.*

they were thinking, Jesus took a child and stood him by his side. [48] He said to the disciples, "Whoever welcomes this child in my name, welcomes me; and whoever welcomes me, welcomes the One who sent me. For he who is least among you all is the greatest."

[49] John replied, "Master, we saw someone casting out demons in your name, and we stopped him, because he was not following with us".

[50] But Jesus said to him, "Don't stop him. For whoever is not against you is for you."

Jesus Begins his Final Journey, South to Jerusalem

[51] When the time was drawing near for him to be taken up, he set himself to go to Jerusalem. [52] He sent messengers to go before him, and they went into a Samaritan[†] town to prepare for his arrival. [53] The Samaritans, however, would not welcome him, because he had set himself to go to Jerusalem.

[54] When the disciples James and John saw this, they said, "Lord, do you want us to call fire down from heaven and destroy them?" [55] But Jesus turned and rebuked them; [56] and they went into another town.

[57] As they went on their way, a certain man said to him, "I will follow you wherever you go".

[58] But Jesus said to him, "Foxes have holes, and birds have nests, but the Son of Man has nowhere to lay his head".

[59] Jesus said to someone else, "Follow me". But he replied, "Lord, first allow me to go and bury my father".

[60] Jesus said to him, "Let the dead bury their own dead; but you go and proclaim the kingdom of God".

[61] Someone else also said to him, "I will follow you, Lord, but first allow me to say goodbye to my family".

---

† Samaria lay on the way south to Judea and Jerusalem from Galilee. The Samaritans had a hostile relationship with the Jews.

[62] Jesus replied, "No-one who puts his hand to the plough and looks back is fit for the kingdom of God".

Chapter 10

[1] After this, the Lord appointed seventy others, and sent them in pairs before him into all the cities and towns where he was about to go. [2] He said to them, "The harvest is large, but the workers are few; therefore, beg the Lord of the harvest to send out workers into his harvest. [3] Go on your way. But watch out—I send you like lambs into the midst of wolves. [4] Do not take a wallet with you, nor a bag, nor sandals; and do not greet anyone on the road. [5] And when you enter a house, first say, 'Peace be on this house'; [6] and if a son of peace is already there, your peace will rest on him; but if not, your word will return to you unused. [7] Remain in his house, eating and drinking what they provide, for the worker deserves his wage. Do not go about from house to house.

[8] "And when you go into a city and they welcome you, eat what they set before you, [9] and heal the sick there and tell them, 'The kingdom of God is near you.' [10] But if you enter a city and they do not welcome you, go out into its streets and say, [11] 'We even wipe off the dust that clings to our feet from your city! But know this: the kingdom of God is near.' [12] I say to you that it will be more tolerable for Sodom on the day of judgement than for that city.

[13] "Woe to you, Chorazin; woe to you, Bethsaida! For if the powerful deeds that have happened in you had taken place in Tyre and Sidon long ago, they would have repented in sackcloth and ashes. [14] But it will be more tolerable for Tyre and Sidon in the judgement than for you. [15] And you, Capernaum, will you be lifted up to the heavens? No, you will go down to hell.

[16] "The one who listens to you, listens to me; and the one who despises you, despises me. But the one who despises me, despises the One who

sent me."

[17] The seventy returned joyfully, saying, "Lord, even the demons submitted to us in your name!"

[18] And he said to them, "I have watched Satan fall, like lightning from the sky. [19] See, I have given you authority to trample over snakes and scorpions and every power of the enemy, and absolutely nothing will harm you. [20] But rejoice not so much that the spirits submit to you, but that your names have been written in heaven."

[21] At that very time[†], he rejoiced in the Holy Spirit and said, "I thank you, Father, Lord of heaven and earth, because you have hidden these things from the wise and intelligent, and have revealed them to children. Yes, Father, because this was how it pleased you to do it. [22] All things have been handed over to me by my Father, and no-one knows who the Son is, except the Father; or who the Father is except the Son, and to whomever the Son decides to reveal him."

[23] And turning to his disciples, he said to them privately, "Blessed are the eyes that see what you see. [24] For I tell you that many prophets and kings wanted to see what you see, but never did; and to hear what you hear, but never did."

[25] Just then, a certain religious lawyer stood up, wanting to test Jesus. "Teacher", he said, "What must I do so that I will inherit eternal life?"

[26] And he said to him, "What is written in the Law? How do you read it?"

[27] The lawyer replied, "Love the Lord your God with all your heart and with all your soul and with all your strength and with all your mind; and love your neighbour as yourself".

[28] Jesus said to him, "You have answered correctly. Do this, and you will live."

[29] But the lawyer wanted to justify himself; so he said to Jesus, "And who is my neighbour?"

[30] In reply, Jesus said, "A certain man was going from Jerusalem to Jericho, when he was ambushed by robbers. They stripped him and beat him and left him half-dead.

[31] "Now by chance, a certain priest was going down that road, but when he saw the man he passed by on the other side. [32] Likewise, a Levite also came to the place, but seeing the man, he passed by on the other side. [33] Then a certain Samaritan who was travelling came to the place, and when he saw the man, he was moved with compassion. [34] He went over to him and bound his wounds, pouring oil and wine on them. Then the Samaritan lifted the wounded man onto his own animal, took him to an inn, and took care of him.

[35] "The next day, he took out two day's wages[†] and gave them to the inn-keeper, and said, 'Take care of him. And whatever more you might spend, I will pay you when I return.'

[36] "Now which of these three, do you think, proved to be a neighbour to the man who was ambushed by robbers?"

[37] The lawyer said, "The one who showed him mercy".

Jesus said to him, "You go and do the same".

[38] As they were travelling, he came into a certain town. A woman named Martha welcomed him into her home, [39] and she had a sister called Mary. Now Mary was sitting at the Lord's feet to listen to what he was saying, [40] but Martha was worried about the many things she had to do to serve her guest. She came up and said, "Lord, don't you care that my sister is leaving me to serve on my own? Tell her to come and help me."

[41] But the Lord answered her, "Martha, Martha, you are anxious and bothered about many things, [42] but there is only one thing that is necessary. For Mary chose the better thing, and it will not be taken away from her."

---

† Literally, *in that same hour.*

† That is, *two denarii.*

Chapter 11

[1] On one occasion, while Jesus was in a certain place and had just finished praying, one of his disciples said to him, "Lord, teach us to pray, like John taught his disciples".

[2] He said to them, "When you pray, say:
'Father,
may your name be made holy[†],
may your kingdom come,
[3] give us each day our daily bread[††],
[4] and forgive us our sins, for we ourselves forgive everyone who is indebted to us;
and do not bring us into testing'".[*]

[5] And he said to them, "Imagine one of you has a friend, and you go to him at midnight and say, 'Friend, lend me three loaves of bread, [6] because my friend has arrived after a journey, and I have nothing to put before him'. [7] And the one inside says, 'Stop disturbing me. The door is already locked, and my children are with me in bed. I can't get up and give you anything'. [8] "I tell you, even though he will not get up and give you bread because he is your friend, yet because of your persistence, he will get up and give you as much as you need.

[9] "And so I tell you, ask and it will be given to you; seek and you will find; knock and it will be opened to you. [10] For everyone who asks receives, and he who seeks finds, and to him who knocks, the door will be opened. [11] If your son asks for a fish, which of you fathers will give him a snake instead? [12] Or if he asks for an egg, will give him a scorpion? [13] If you, then, who are evil, know how to give good gifts to your children, how much more will the Father give from heaven the Holy Spirit to those who ask him?"

[14] Now he was driving out a demon that was mute. And as the demon came out, the man who had been mute spoke, and the crowds were astonished. [15] But some of them said, "It is by Beelzebul, the prince of demons, that he drives out the demons". [16] Others, wanting to test him, kept asking him to perform a sign from heaven.

[17] But Jesus knew their thoughts, and said to them, "Every kingdom that is divided against itself comes to ruin; and every house against a house falls. [18] If Satan also is divided against himself, how will his kingdom stand? For you say, 'By Beelzebul he drives out the demons', [19] but if I drive out the demons by Beelzebul, by whom do your sons drive them out? On account of this, they will be your judges.

[20] "However, if it is by the finger of God that I drive out the demons, then surely the kingdom of God has overtaken you. [21] When a strong, fully-armed man guards his own house, his possessions are secure. [22] But when a stronger man comes along and defeats him, he takes from him all the armour in which he trusted, and divides up the spoils.

[23] "He who is not with me is against me, and he who does not gather with me, scatters. [24] Whenever an unclean spirit comes out of a person, it passes through dry places seeking rest, and does not find any. Then it says, 'I will return to the house I came out of'. [25] And coming back, it finds it all swept clean and in order. [26] Then it goes and gets seven other spirits more evil than itself, and goes in to live there. And that person ends up worse off than he was at the beginning."

[27] Now while he was saying these things, a woman from the crowd called out, "Blessed is the womb which bore you, and the breasts which nursed you".

[28] But Jesus said, "Blessed rather are those who hear the message of God, and keep it".

[29] With the crowds increasing around him, he began to speak: "This generation is an evil generation. It seeks a sign; but no sign will be given to it except the sign of Jonah. [30] For just as Jonah was a sign to the Ninevites, so also the Son of Man will be to this generation. [31] The Queen of

---

† Traditionally, *hallowed by your name.*
†† Literally, *give us each day our bread for tomorrow.*
* Or *temptation.*

Sheba will rise up at the judgement with the men of this generation and condemn them, because she came from the ends of the earth to hear the wisdom of Solomon. Yet something greater than Solomon is here. [32] The men of Nineveh will rise in the judgement with this generation, and condemn it, because they repented at the preaching of Jonah. Yet something greater than Jonah is here.

[33] "No-one lights a lamp only to put it in a cellar; instead, it is put on the lampstand, so that those who enter may see its light. [34] The lamp of the body is your eye. When your eye is healthy[†] to others, your whole body is full of light; but when your eye is evil[††], then your body is dark. [35] See to it, then, that the light within you is not darkness. [36] If, therefore, your whole body is full of light, with no part dark, it will be as full of light as when the lamp shines out brilliantly upon you."

[37] While he was speaking, a Pharisee invited Jesus to have dinner with him; and Jesus went into the Pharisee's house and reclined at the table. [38] When the Pharisee saw this, he was astonished, because Jesus did not first ritually wash himself before dinner. [39] The Lord said to him, "Now you Pharisees cleanse the outside of the cup and the plate, but on the inside you are full of greed and wickedness. [40] O you fools—did not he who made the outside make the inside as well? [41] Instead, give the contents of the cup and plate to the poor, and you will find that all things are clean for you.

[42] "But woe to you Pharisees, because you give a tenth of your mint and rue and all your herbs, but you overlook justice and the love of God. You should have done these things, without neglecting the others.

[43] "Woe to you Pharisees, because you love the best seat in the synagogues, and the way people greet you in the market place. [44] Woe to you, because you are like an unmarked grave which those walking above do not realise is there."

[45] One of the religious lawyers answered him, "Teacher, you insult us as well by saying these things".

[46] But Jesus said, "Woe to you religious lawyers as well! For you load people up with burdens that are hard to carry, but you yourselves will not lift one finger to bear the load. [47] Woe to you, because you build the tombs of the prophets, but your fathers were the ones who killed them! [48] Therefore, you are witnesses and accessories to the deeds of your fathers, because they killed the prophets and you yourselves build their tombs. [49] It is for this reason that the Wisdom of God said, 'I will send them prophets and apostles; and they will kill and persecute some of them', [50] so that this generation might be blamed for the blood of all the prophets that has been shed since the foundation of the world—[51] from the blood of Abel through to the blood of Zechariah, who died between the altar and the sanctuary. Yes, I tell you it will be blamed on this generation!

[52] "Woe to you religious lawyers, because you hold the key to knowledge; you yourselves will not go inside, and you get in the way of those who do want to go in."

[53] And as he left there, the Scribes and Pharisees began to be very resentful, and to attack him with all kinds of questions, [54] hoping all the time to catch him out in something he might say.

Chapter 12

[1] Meanwhile, a crowd of many thousands had gathered so that the people were actually trampling on one another.

Jesus began to speak first to his disciples: "Beware of the 'yeast' of the Pharisees, by which I mean their hypocrisy. [2] There is nothing which has been concealed that will not in the future be

---

†   The Greek word here also means *generous*.
†† To have an *evil eye* was a Jewish way of saying *miserly* or *stingy*.

revealed, and nothing secret that will not be made known. ³ So, whatever you have said in the dark will be heard in the light, and what you have whispered in the privacy of your home will be proclaimed from the housetops.

⁴ "To you my friends I say, do not fear those who kill the body and afterwards can do nothing more. ⁵ Let me warn you about whom you should fear: fear him who, after the killing, has authority to cast into hell. Yes, I tell you, fear him!

⁶ "Are not five sparrows sold for just a small amount?† Yet not one of them is forgotten in God's sight. ⁷ But even the hairs on your head have all been counted. Do not fear; you are worth more than many sparrows.

⁸ "And I tell you, everyone who acknowledges me before other people, the Son of Man will acknowledge before the angels of God. ⁹ But the person who disowns me before other people will be disowned before the angels of God. ¹⁰ And everyone who speaks a word against the Son of Man will be forgiven for it; but the one who insults†† the Holy Spirit will not be forgiven.

¹¹ "Now, when they bring you before the synagogues, the leaders and the authorities, do not be anxious about how or by what you will defend yourselves, or what you will say. ¹² For the Holy Spirit will instruct you in that moment about the things you should say."

¹³ Then someone out of the crowd said to him, "Teacher, tell my brother to divide the family inheritance with me."

¹⁴ But Jesus said to him, "Sir, who appointed me as judge or arbiter for both of you?" ¹⁵ And he said to the crowd, "Watch out and be on your guard against every type of greed, because one's life does not consist in the abundance of possessions".

¹⁶ And then he told them a parable: "The land of a certain wealthy man produced a good harvest, ¹⁷ and he thought to himself, 'What will I do, since I have nowhere to store my crops?' ¹⁸ Then he said, 'This is what I will do. I will knock down my existing barns and build bigger ones, and there I will store all my grain and goods. ¹⁹ And I will say to my soul, "Soul, you have many good things laid up for many years to come. Relax; eat, drink and celebrate."'

²⁰ "But God said to him, 'You fool! This very night your soul is demanded back from you. And the things you have prepared—whose will they be then?'

²¹ "This is how it will be with those who store up things for themselves, but are not rich towards God."

²² Then he said to the disciples, "Therefore I tell you, do not be anxious about your life—what you will eat; nor about your body—what you will wear. ²³ For your life is more than food, and your body is more than clothing. ²⁴ Think of the crows and how they do not sow or harvest; nor do they have a storehouse or a barn, and yet God provides for them. How much more valuable you are than the birds! ²⁵ And which of you by your anxiety can add a single moment to your life span? ²⁶ So if you cannot achieve such a small thing, why are you anxious about the rest? ²⁷ Think about how the lilies grow. They do not work or make clothes. But I tell you, not even King Solomon in all his glory was dressed like one of these. ²⁸ Now if this is the way God clothes the grass in the field, which grows today and is thrown into the incinerator tomorrow, how much more will he clothe you—people of little faith!

²⁹ "And do not strive† after what you will eat and drink, or be worried. ³⁰ For these are the things all the nations of the world strive after, and your Father knows that you need them. ³¹ Instead, strive for his kingdom, and these other things will be given to you as well. ³² Do not fear, little flock, for it is your Father's pleasure to give you the kingdom.

---

†   Literally, *two assaria*.
††   Traditionally, *blasphemes*.

†   Or *seek*; also below.

[33] "Sell your possessions and give to the poor. Make for yourselves money bags that will not wear out; a never-ending treasure in heaven, where no thief comes close, and no moth destroys. [34] For where your 'treasure' is, that's where your heart will be also.

[35] "Be dressed ready for work and have your lamps lit; [36] be like people who are expecting their master to return from a banquet, so that when he comes and knocks on the door they open it immediately.

[37] "Blessed are those servants whom the master finds alert when he returns. Truly I tell you, he will dress himself ready to work, have them recline at the table and wait on them! [38] Blessed are those servants, if he comes at midnight or four in the morning and finds them alert.

[39] "Now understand this: if the householder had known what time the thief would come, he would not have let him break into the house. [40] You also be ready, because the Son of Man is coming at a time you would not imagine."

[41] Peter said, "Lord, are you saying this parable for us or for everyone?"

[42] The Lord replied, "Who, then, is the faithful and wise manager whom the master will appoint over his staff to give them a food allowance at the proper time? [43] Blessed is that servant whom the master finds doing this task when he comes. [44] Truly I say to you, he will appoint that one over all his possessions. [45] But if that servant says in his heart, 'My master is delayed in coming', and so begins to beat the other servants and maids, and to eat and drink and get drunk, [46] then that servant's master will arrive on a day he does not expect, and at an hour he does not know. The master will cut him in half and assign him a place with the unfaithful.

[47] "That servant who knows his master's wishes and does not prepare for or perform his wishes, will receive a great beating. [48] But the one who does not know his wishes and yet does what is worthy of punishment will receive a light beating.

From everyone who has been given much, much will be expected. And from the one who has been entrusted with much, even more will be asked.

[49] "I have come to bring a fire upon the earth, and how I wish it were burning already. [50] I have a baptism to experience and how distressed I am until it is achieved. [51] Do you suppose that I have come to establish peace in the world? No, I tell you, but rather division! [52] From now on, five people in one home will be divided: three against two, and two against three; [53] they will be divided, father against son, and son against father, mother against daughter, and daughter against mother, mother-in-law against her daughter-in-law, and daughter-in-law against mother-in-law."

[54] Now he also said to the crowds, "When you see a cloud rising in the west, immediately you say, 'A rainstorm is coming', and so it does. [55] And when a south wind blows you say, 'A heat-wave will come', and so it does. [56] You hypocrites! You know how to interpret the appearance of the earth and sky, but why don't you know how to interpret the current time. [57] Why also do you not judge for yourselves what is right? [58] So as you are going with your opponent to the ruler, make an effort to settle things with him, so that he will not drag you off to the judge, and the judge hand you over to the guard, and the guard throw you into prison. [59] I say to you, you will certainly not get out from there until you have repaid the very last coin!"

Chapter 13

[1] Some of those present at that time told Jesus about the people from Galilee whose blood Pilate[†] had mixed with their sacrifices. [2] Jesus responded, "Do you think that these Galileans were worse sinners than all the other Galileans just because they suffered these things? [3] No, I

---

† That is, Pontius Pilate, the Roman Governor of Judea.

tell you, but if you do not repent, similarly you will all perish. [4] Or those eighteen people upon whom the tower in Siloam fell and killed them—do you think that they were more guilty than all the other people living in Jerusalem? [5] No, I tell you, but if you do not repent, likewise you will all perish."

[6] Then he told this parable: "A man had a figtree planted in his vineyard; he came to it looking for fruit but found none. [7] Then he said to the gardener, 'Look, I have come looking for fruit on this figtree for three years, yet I find none. Cut it down. Why should it even waste the soil?' [8] But the gardener answered, 'Lord, please leave it also for one more year, until I can dig around it and fertilise it. [9] It may yet produce fruit; but if it does not, by all means, you can cut it down.'"

[10] Now Jesus was teaching in one of the synagogues on the Sabbath Day. [11] There was a woman present who suffered from a spirit of illness for eighteen years; she was doubled over and was unable to stand up straight. [12] When Jesus saw her, he called her over and said, "Dear woman, be released from your illness". [13] He laid his hands on her and immediately she straightened up and began glorifying God.

[14] But the synagogue-leader was annoyed that Jesus had healed on the Sabbath Day, and responded by saying to the crowd, "There are six days in which work should be done, so come and be healed on one of those days, not on the Sabbath Day!"

[15] But the Lord replied, "You hypocrites! Don't each of you on the Sabbath release your ox or donkey from the feeding trough and lead it away for a drink? [16] This woman is a daughter of Abraham. She has been imprisoned by Satan for eighteen years. Should she not be released from this prison on the Sabbath Day?"

[17] In saying these things, those who opposed him were humiliated, yet the entire crowd was overjoyed because of the wonderful things he was doing.

[18] So he said, "What is God's Kingdom like and to what could I compare it? [19] It is like a mustard seed that someone took and threw into his garden. It grew and became a tree and the birds of the air nested in its branches." [20] Again he said, "To what could I compare God's Kingdom? [21] It is like yeast that a woman took and mixed into a large amount of flour until the whole batch of dough was leavened."

[22] Jesus was travelling through various cities and towns, teaching in them, as he continued his journey toward Jerusalem.

[23] Someone asked him, "Lord, will only a small number of people be rescued?" And he replied to them, [24] "Strive to enter the narrow door. For, I tell you, once the house owner gets up and locks the door, many will attempt to enter and will not be able. [25] You may all stand outside and begin to knock on the door, saying, 'Lord, open up for us!' But he will say in reply, 'I do not remember you people or where you're from'. [26] Then you will begin to say, 'We ate and drank with you and you taught in our streets'. [27] But he will say to you, 'I do not remember where you come from. Get away from me, you who have committed injustices!' [28] In that place there will be weeping and grinding of teeth, when you see Abraham and Isaac and Jacob and all the prophets inside the kingdom of God, but you people thrown out of it. [29] Yet, people from east and west, from north and south, will come and recline at the dining table in the kingdom of God. [30] Indeed, some who are now last will be first, and some who are now first will be last."

[31] At that very time, some Pharisees came to Jesus saying, "Depart from here and move on, because King Herod is looking to kill you".

[32] He replied, "Go tell that fox, 'Listen, I will continue to cast out demons and perform healings today and tomorrow, and on the third day I will be brought to my goal. [33] But I must keep moving on today and tomorrow and the next day, because it is unthinkable that a prophet would be killed out-

side of Jerusalem.' [34] Jerusalem, Jerusalem, the city which kills the prophets and stones those sent to her! How often I have wanted to gather your children as a hen gathers her own chicks under her wing, yet you were not willing. [35] Look, your house is left abandoned. I tell you, you will not see me until the time comes when you declare, 'Blessed is the one who comes in the name of the Lord.'"

Chapter 14

[1] One Sabbath Day, Jesus was going to the home of a leading Pharisee to eat a meal, and they were watching him. [2] Right then a man came to him who was suffering from oedema.[†] [3] Jesus asked the religious lawyers and the Pharisees, "Is it proper to heal on the Sabbath, or not?" [4] But they kept silent. So Jesus took hold of the man, healed him, and helped him on his way. [5] Then he said to them, "If your son or your ox fell into a pit on the Sabbath, who among you would not pull him out straight away?" [6] And they were not able to give a reply to this.

[7] When he arrived, he noticed how they all chose to sit at the places of honour. So he told a parable to the guests: [8] "When you are invited by someone to a banquet, do not recline at the places of honour in case someone more esteemed than you has been invited by the host. [9] The one who invited you both may come and say to you, 'Give this person your place'. And then in disgrace you will move to the last place. [10] But when you are invited, make your way to the last place, so that when your host comes he may say to you, 'Friend, move up to a more esteemed place'. Then you will be honoured before everyone sitting at the table with you. [11] For everyone who exalts himself will be humbled, and the one who humbles himself will be exalted."

[12] Then Jesus said to his host, "When you put on a lunch or dinner, do not call your friends or your colleagues or your family members or wealthy neighbours, in case they return the invitation and you would be repaid. [13] Instead, when you put on a banquet, invite the poor, the disabled, the crippled and the blind. [14] Then you will be blessed because they do not have the means to repay you. Indeed, you will be repaid at the resurrection of the righteous."

[15] On hearing this, one of those at the table said to Jesus, "Blessed is the person who will share a meal in the kingdom of God". [16] So Jesus said to him, "A certain man organized a large dinner and invited many guests. [17] At the time for the dinner, he sent his servant to say to the guests, 'Come along, for the meal is already prepared'. [18] One after another, they all began to make excuses. The first one said to him, 'I have just bought a field and I must go out to see it. Please have me excused'. [19] Another said, 'I have just bought five yoke of oxen and I am going to inspect them. Please have me excused'. [20] Another said, 'I have just married a girl and so am not able to attend'. [21] The servant went back and reported these things to his master.

"The master of the home was furious and said to his servant, 'Go out quickly into the streets and lane-ways of the city and bring in the poor, the disabled, the blind and lame'.

[22] "Then the servant said, 'Master, what you have ordered has been done, yet there is still some room'.

[23] "The master said to the servant, 'Go out into the highways and country lanes and convince them to come in, so that my home may be filled. [24] For I tell you, not one of those people I previously invited will have a taste of my dinner'".

[25] Now, great crowds of people were travelling along with Jesus. He turned around and said to them, [26] "If anyone comes to me and does not hate his own father, mother, wife, children, brothers and sisters, and even his own life, he is not

---

†   Traditionally 'dropsy'. A medical condition characterized by an excess of watery fluid causing swelling.

able to be my disciple. [27] Whoever does not carry his own cross and come after me is not able to be my disciple. [28] For who among you would plan to build a tower and not first sit down and calculate the cost; whether you have enough to complete it? [29] Otherwise, you may lay the foundation and not be able to finish it. And everyone who sees it would begin to mock you: [30] 'This person began to build yet is unable to finish it'. [31] Or what king would go out to meet another king in battle, and not first sit down to consider whether he is able with ten thousand soldiers to confront the one who brings twenty thousand against him? [32] If he is not able, then while the other is still far away he would send out representatives to ask for terms of peace. [33] Therefore, in the same way, everyone of you who does not give up all that you have is not able to be my disciple.

[34] "So then, salt is good; but if it becomes tasteless, how can it possibly be made salty again? [35] It is not suitable for the soil or the compost heap; people simply throw it away. Let anyone with ears to hear, listen!"

Chapter 15

[1] Now all the tax collectors and sinners were drawing close to listen to Jesus. [2] But the Pharisees and the Scribes were grumbling and saying, "This man welcomes sinners and eats meals with them". [3] So he told them this parable:

[4] "What man among you, if he owned a hundred sheep and lost one of them, would not leave the ninety-nine in the desert and go after the lost one until he found it? [5] And when he had found it, he would lay it upon his shoulders and be overjoyed. [6] Returning home, he would call together his friends and neighbours and say to them, 'Rejoice with me because I have found my lost sheep!' [7] I tell you, in the same way there will be more joy in heaven on account of one sinner who repents than over ninety-nine righteous people who do not need repentance.

[8] "Or again, what woman if she owned ten silver coins and lost one of them, would not light a lamp, sweep her home, and search thoroughly until she found it? [9] And when she found it, she would call together her girlfriends and neighbours and say, 'Rejoice with me because I have found the lost silver coin!' [10] In the same way, I tell you, there is joy in the presence of God's angels on account of one sinner who repents."

[11] Jesus continued: "There was a man who had two sons. [12] The younger one said to his father, 'Father, give me my share of the inheritance'. The father then divided the estate between the two sons. [13] Soon afterwards, the younger son collected everything together and took off to a distant land, where he squandered his inheritance on reckless living. [14] After he had spent everything, there was a great famine in that land, and he began to be in need. [15] So he went and hired himself out to a citizen of that land, who sent him out to his fields to feed pigs. [16] And he was longing to feed himself with the pods that the pigs were eating; yet no-one gave him anything. [17] Then he came to his senses and thought, 'How many of my father's employees have an abundance of food, and yet here am I dying of hunger. [18] I'll get up and go to my father and say to him, 'I have sinned toward God[†] and before you. [19] I am no longer worthy to be called your son. Make me like one of your employees.' [20] So he got up and went to his father.

"He was still some distance away when his father caught sight of him. The father was deeply moved, and running to his son he embraced him and kissed him. [21] The son said, 'Father, I have sinned toward God and before you. I am no longer worthy to be called your son.'

[22] "But the father said to his servants, 'Quick, bring out the best robe and dress him in it; put a ring on his finger and shoes on his feet. [23] Bring

---

†   Literally, *heaven*, and below.

the fattened calf and kill it. Let's eat and cele-brate, [24] because this son of mine was dead but is now alive again; he was lost but is now found.' And they began to celebrate.

[25] "Now the elder son had been in the field, and as he drew near the house he heard music and dancing. [26] And calling one of the hired-hands, he asked what this was all about. [27] He replied, 'Your brother has come and your father has killed the fattened calf, because he has got him back safely'. [28] The elder son became furious and refused even to enter the house. But his father went outside and pleaded with him. [29] He answered his father, 'Look here! I have been serv-ing you for so many years and have never neg-lected your instructions. Yet you have never even given me a goat so that I may have a celebration with my friends. [30] Now when this son of yours, who has wasted your estate on prostitutes, comes home, you kill the fattened calf for him.'

[31] "But the father said to him, 'My child, you are always with me, and everything that is mine is yours. [32] But we must celebrate and rejoice, because this brother of yours was dead but is now alive, and was lost but is now found.'"

Chapter 16

[1] Jesus also said to the disciples, "There was a cer-tain rich man who had a manager. This manager was accused of wasting his master's resources, [2] and so the rich man called him in and said, 'What is this that I hear about you? Give me back your management accounts, for you cannot be my manager any longer.'

[3] "The manager said to himself, 'What am I going to do, for my master is about to take my job away from me? I am not strong enough to dig, and I am ashamed to beg. [4] Ah, I know what I should do, so that when I have been removed from being manager, people will welcome me into their homes.'

[5] "And he called in each of his master's debtors, one at a time. He said to the first, 'How much do you owe my master?' [6] He replied, '100 drums of oil'. So the manager said to him, 'Take your bill, sit down quickly and make it 50'.

[7] "Then he said to another, 'How much do you owe?' And he replied, '100 measures of wheat'. He said to him, 'Take your bill and make it 80'.

[8] "Now the master commended the unright-eous manager because he had acted cleverly. You see, the sons of this age are cleverer than the sons of light, when it comes to dealing with their own kind. [9] And so I tell you, make friends for yourselves with unrighteous money so that when it fails, they will welcome you into eternal dwellings.

[10] "The one who is faithful with very little will also be faithful with much; and the one who is unrighteous with very little, will also be unrighteous with much. [11] If then, you have not been faithful with unrighteous money, who will entrust you with true riches? [12] And if you have not been faithful with what belongs to someone else, who will give you things of your own? [13] No servant can serve two masters. For he will hate one and love the other; or he will cling onto one and despise the other. You cannot serve God and Money."

[14] The Pharisees (who loved money) were lis-tening to all this, and mocking him.

[15] So Jesus said to them, "You are those who justify yourselves before other people, but God knows your hearts; for things which people value highly are detestable in God's sight. [16] The Law and the Prophets were in place until John came. Since then, the kingdom of God is being announced and everyone is reacting violently towards it; [17] but it would be easier for heaven and earth to pass away than for the smallest stroke of the law to fall. [18] Everyone who divorces his wife and marries another, commits adultery; and the man that marries the divorced woman also commits adultery.

¹⁹ "There was a certain rich man who used to wear the finest clothes and hold magnificent parties every day. ²⁰ A poor man named Lazarus, who was covered in sores, lay ill at his front gate. ²¹ And Lazarus longed to satisfy his hunger from the scraps that fell from the rich man's table. Not only so, but the dogs used to come and lick his sores.

²² "Now eventually Lazarus died and was carried by the angels to the side of Abraham.† The rich man also died and was buried. ²³ And being in the place of the dead and in torment, he looked up and saw Abraham at a great distance, with Lazarus by his side.

²⁴ "He screamed, 'Father Abraham, be merciful to me! Send Lazarus to dip the tip of his finger in some water to cool my tongue, for I am in agony in this fire.'

²⁵ "But Abraham replied, 'My child, remember that you received your good things in your lifetime, and in the same way Lazarus received bad things. Now he is comforted here, but you are in agony. ²⁶ And in any case, between us and you a great chasm has been established, so that those who want to go over from here to you are not able to; nor is it possible to cross over from there to us.'

²⁷ "He replied, 'Then, I beg you, Father, to send Lazarus to my father's house, ²⁸ for I have five brothers. He could warn them so that they might not also come to this place of torment.'

²⁹ "Abraham replied, 'They have Moses and the Prophets. Let them listen to them.'

³⁰ "But the rich man said, 'No, Father Abraham! But if someone were to go to them from the dead, they would repent.'

³¹ "He replied, 'If they do not listen to Moses and the Prophets, they will not be persuaded even if someone rises from the dead'".

---

† A euphemism for being brought into God's presence (or heaven).

Chapter 17

¹ Jesus said to his disciples, "It is inevitable that stumbling blocks should come, but woe to the person through whom it comes. ² He would be better off having a mill-stone tied round his neck and being thrown into the sea than to cause one of these little ones to stumble. ³ Watch yourselves closely. If your brother sins, rebuke him; and if he repents, forgive him. ⁴ Even if he sins against you seven times in a single day, and seven times turns back to you and says, 'I repent', then you are to forgive him."

⁵ And the apostles said to the Lord, "Increase our faith!"

⁶ But the Lord said, "If you have faith even as small as a mustard seed, you can say to a mulberry tree, 'Be uprooted and planted in the sea', and it will obey you.

⁷ "Imagine you have a servant to plough the field or look after the sheep. When he comes in from the field, which of you would say to him, 'Come at once, and recline at the table'? ⁸ No, you would say to him, 'Prepare my dinner and dress yourself to wait on me while I dine, and afterwards you may eat and drink'. ⁹ Do you thank the servant for doing what he was commanded to do? ¹⁰ It is the same with you. When you have done everything you have been commanded, you should say, 'We are unworthy servants; we have only done what we were supposed to'".

¹¹ On the way to Jerusalem, Jesus was passing through the border region between Samaria and Galilee. ¹² As he entered one particular town, they met ten lepers, standing at a distance. ¹³ The lepers called out, "Jesus, Master, be merciful to us!"

¹⁴ And when Jesus saw them, he replied, "Go and show yourselves to the priests". And while they were going, they were made clean.

¹⁵ When one of them realised that he had been healed, he came back, glorifying God in a loud voice. ¹⁶ He fell on his face at Jesus' feet, and thanked him. And he was a Samaritan.

¹⁷ Jesus responded, "Weren't there ten who

were made clean? Where are the other nine? [18] Did none come back to give glory to God except this foreigner?" [19] And he said to him, "Stand up, and go on your way. Your faith has rescued you."

[20] Once, when he had been asked by the Pharisees when the kingdom of God was coming, he replied, "The coming of God's kingdom is something that can not be closely observed; [21] nor will they say, 'Look it is here, or there'. For the kingdom of God is in your midst."

[22] He said to the disciples, "Days are coming when you will long to see one of the days of the Son of Man, and you will not see it. [23] And they will say, 'Look it is there! Look it is here!' Do not go; and do not follow them. [24] For the Son of Man will be like flashes of lightning that light up the sky from one horizon to the other. [25] But first he must suffer many things and be rejected by this generation. [26] In the days of the Son of Man, it will be just as it was in the days of Noah— [27] they were eating, drinking, marrying and giving in marriage, until the day Noah entered the ark, and the flood came and destroyed them all. [28] A similar thing happened in the days of Lot— people were eating, drinking, buying, selling, planting and building. [29] But on the day Lot left Sodom, fire and sulfur rained from heaven, and destroyed them all. [30] It will be just the same on the day when the Son of Man is revealed. [31] On that day, no-one who is on the roof should go down into his house to get his belongings; and likewise, no-one who is in the field should turn back. [32] Remember Lot's wife. [33] Whoever tries to preserve his life will lose it; but whoever loses it will keep it alive.

[34] "I say to you, on that night, two men will be reclining on one couch at the table—one will be taken and the other left. [35] Two women will be grinding grain together—one will be taken but the other left." [†]

---

† Some ancient manuscripts add: " [36] Two men will be in a field—one will be taken but the other left."

[37] They answered him, "Where Lord?" And he said to them, "Where the body is, there the vultures gather".

Chapter 18

[1] Then Jesus told them a parable to the effect that they should always pray and not give up. [2] He said, "In a certain city there was a judge who had no reverence for God and no respect for other people. [3] Now there was a widow in that city, who would come to him saying, 'Please help me get justice over my opponent'.

[4] "For some time he was not willing to help. But later he said to himself, 'Though I do not have reverence for God nor respect for other people, [5] yet because this widow is troubling me I will help her get justice. Otherwise, in the end, her constant approaches will wear me out.'"

[6] Then the Lord said, "Listen to what the unjust judge says. [7] Will not God, then, achieve justice for his chosen people, who cry out to him day and night? Does he delay in helping them? [8] I tell you, he will achieve justice for them quickly. Yet when the Son of Man comes, will he find such faithfulness on the earth?"

[9] To some who were self-confident, considering themselves to be righteous and having contempt for the rest, he also told this parable: [10] "Two people went up to the temple to pray. One was a Pharisee, the other a tax collector. [11] The Pharisee took his stand and was praying about himself, 'God, I thank you that I am not the same as the rest of humanity: swindlers, unrighteous, adulterers, or even like this tax collector. [12] I fast two days a week; I give away a tenth of everything I earn.'

[13] "But the tax collector stood at a distance and would not look up to heaven. Instead, he beat his chest and said, 'God, please be merciful to me, the sinner!' [14] I tell you, this man went home with God having considered him righteous.

The other man did not. For everyone who exalts himself will be humbled, but everyone who humbles himself will be exalted."

[15] People were bringing infants to Jesus so that he might touch them. When they saw this, the disciples rebuked them. [16] But Jesus summoned them and said, "Allow the children to come to me; do not prevent them. For the kingdom of God is for ones like this. [17] Truly, I tell you, whoever does not accept God's kingdom like a child does, will not enter it."

[18] A certain leader asked him, "Good teacher, what should I do to inherit eternal life?"

[19] Jesus said to him, "Why do you speak of me as 'good'? No-one is good except God alone. [20] You know the commandments: do not commit adultery; do not murder; do not steal; do not give false evidence; honour your father and mother."

[21] He replied, "I have kept all these things since my youth".

[22] When Jesus heard this, he said to him, "You still lack one thing. Sell everything you have and give the proceeds to the poor, and you will have a treasure in heaven. And come follow me!" [23] But when the man heard this he became distressed; for he was very rich.

[24] When Jesus saw this about him, he said, "How difficult it is for those who have wealth to enter into God's kingdom. [25] Indeed, it is easier for a camel to enter through the eye of a needle than for a rich person to enter God's kingdom."

[26] Those hearing this said, "Then who is able to be rescued?"

[27] Jesus replied, "What is humanly impossible is possible for God".

[28] Then Peter said, "Look, we have left our homes and followed you".

[29] And Jesus replied, "Truly, I tell you, there is no-one who has left house or wife or brothers or parents or children for the sake of God's kingdom [30] who will not receive much, much more in this present age, and eternal life in the age to come".

[31] Then he took the twelve aside and said to them, "Look, we are going up to Jerusalem and everything written by the prophets about the Son of Man will be accomplished. [32] For he will be handed over to people from other nations, and be ridiculed and insulted and spat upon. [33] They will flog him then kill him, and on the third day he will be raised to life." [34] Yet they did not comprehend any of these things; this saying remained hidden from them and they did not understand what was said.

[35] As he approached Jericho, a certain blind man was sitting beside the road begging. [36] When he heard the crowd going by, he asked what was happening. [37] People explained to him that Jesus, the man from Nazareth, was passing by. [38] Then he shouted out, "Jesus, son of King David, be merciful to me".

[39] Those in the front of the crowd rebuked him, insisting that he be quiet. But he cried out all the more, "Son of King David, be merciful to me".

[40] Jesus stopped and ordered the man to be brought to him. As he approached, Jesus asked him, [41] "What do you want me to do for you?"

"Lord", he replied, "I want to see again".

[42] Jesus said to him, "Then see again! Your faith has rescued you."

[43] Immediately, he was able to see again. And he followed after Jesus, glorifying God. When all the people saw this they gave praise to God.

Chapter 19

[1] Jesus entered Jericho and was passing through. [2] There was a man there named Zacchaeus, a senior tax collector who was rich. [3] He was trying to see who Jesus was, but because of the crowd was unable to, for he was a small man. [4] He ran ahead of the crowd, and climbed up a fig tree to see him, because Jesus was about to pass through that way.

[5] When Jesus got to that point, he looked up and said to him, "Zacchaeus, climb down quickly

because I have to stay in your home today". [6] He climbed down quickly and welcomed Jesus gladly into his home.

[7] When everyone saw this, they complained, "He has gone to stay with a man who is a sinner".

[8] But Zacchaeus stood up and said to the Lord, "Look, half of my belongings, Lord, I will give away to the poor. And if I have cheated anyone out of anything, I will repay four times the amount."

[9] Then Jesus said to him, "Today rescue has come to this home, for this man too is now a son of Abraham. [10] For the Son of Man came to seek out and rescue what was lost."

[11] While they were still listening, Jesus went on to tell them a parable, because he was close to Jerusalem and the people were thinking that the kingdom of God was going to appear straight away. [12] He said, "A certain nobleman went to a distant land to receive kingly authority and then return. [13] He called ten of his servants, gave them ten minas[†] and said to them, 'Do business with these while I am gone'.

[14] "However, his citizens hated him and sent a delegation after him saying, 'We do not want this man to reign over us'. [15] Yet he did receive his kingly authority, and when he returned he had those servants to whom he had given money summoned before him, so that he could find out what profit they had made in business.

[16] "The first one came and said, 'Lord, your single mina has earned ten minas'. [17] He said to him, 'Well done good servant; because you have been faithful with a small thing, take authority over ten of my cities'.

[18] "The second came saying, 'Lord, your single mina has made five minas'. [19] And to this one also he said, 'Take authority over five of my cities'.

[20] The other one came saying, 'Look, Lord, here is the single mina I have stored away in a piece of cloth. [21] I was afraid of you, because you are a strict man, taking what you did not deposit and

reaping what you did not sow'. [22] He replied, 'You wicked servant! By the words of your own mouth I will judge you. You knew, did you, that I was a strict man, taking what I did not deposit and reaping what I did not sow? [23] Why then did you not give my money to a bank? At least then, on my return, I could have collected it with some interest'. [24] And he said to those present, 'Take the mina from him and give it to the one who has ten minas'.

[25] "They replied to him, 'Lord, he already has ten minas!'

[26] "And he said, 'I tell you, everyone who has something will be given more; but from the one who has nothing, even what he has will be taken away. [27] But as for those enemies of mine who did not want me to reign over them, bring them here and execute them before me."

[28] After saying these things, Jesus kept moving on up to Jerusalem.

Jesus arrives at Jerusalem

[29] As Jesus neared Bethphage and Bethany, at the place called the Mount of Olives, he sent out two of the disciples, [30] saying, "Go into the town opposite. As you enter, you will find a colt tied up there on which no-one has ever ridden. Untie it and bring it here. [31] If someone asks you, 'Why are you untying the colt?', say 'Because the Lord needs it'."

[32] Those who had been sent went off and found things just as Jesus had told them. [33] As they were untying the colt, its owners said to them, "Why are you untying the colt?" [34] So they said, "Because the Lord needs it".

[35] They brought the animal to Jesus, threw their cloaks over it and got Jesus to sit on it. [36] As he rode along, others spread out their cloaks on the road. [37] Now as he neared the place where the road descends the Mount of Olives, the whole crowd of disciples began to praise God joyfully and loudly because of all the mighty deeds they had seen. [38] They declared, "Blessed be the king who comes in the name of the Lord! Peace in heaven and glory in the highest."

† A 'mina' was about three months wages for a labourer.

[39] Yet some of the Pharisees in the crowd called out to Jesus, "Teacher, rebuke your disciples!"

[40] Jesus replied, "I tell you, if they were to keep quiet, the stones would cry out".

[41] As Jesus came near and saw the city, he wept over it. [42] He said, "How I wish that you—you of all places—had recognized this day the things that bring peace! But now they are hidden from your eyes. [43] For days are coming upon you when your enemies will set up a barricade against your walls. They will surround you and trap you from every side. [44] They will destroy you and your children within your walls, and they will not leave a single stone upon another within you. And all this because you did not recognize the time of your visitation."

[45] Then he entered the temple court and began to drive out those who were selling things there. [46] He said to them, "In the Scriptures it is written, 'My house will be a house of prayer', but you have made it into a hideout for robbers!"

[47] He was teaching daily in the temple court. But the Chief Priests, Scribes and leaders of the people were trying to kill him. [48] Yet they could not find a way to do it, because all the people were hanging on his every word.

Chapter 20

[1] One day, as he was teaching the people in the temple court and announcing the news, the Chief Priests and the Scribes approached him together with the Elders. [2] They said to him, "Tell us, by what authority are you doing these things? Or who is the one who gives you this authority?"

[3] He answered, "I will also ask you something; now you tell me: [4] Was the baptism of John from heaven or of human origin?"

[5] They discussed this among themselves, saying, "If we say, 'From heaven', he will say, 'Then why didn't you believe in him?' [6] But if we say, 'of human origin', all the people will stone us because they are convinced that John was a prophet." [7] And so they answered that they did not know where it was from.

[8] Jesus said to them, "Nor will I tell you by what authority I am doing these things".

[9] He began to tell the people this parable: "A man planted a vineyard and leased it to tenants, and went away for quite some time. [10] After a while, he sent a servant to the tenants so that they might give him his share of the vineyard's produce. But the tenants beat the servant and sent him away with nothing. [11] Then he sent another servant, but they beat him also, treated him shamefully and sent him away with nothing. [12] Then he sent a third one but they hurt him also, and cast him out.

[13] "Now the master of the vineyard said, 'What will I do? I will send my beloved son; perhaps they will respect him.'

[14] "But when the tenants saw him they reasoned with one another, 'This is the heir. Let's kill him so that the inheritance will be ours.' [15] So they threw him out of the vineyard and killed him.

"So then, what will the master of the vineyard do to them? [16] He will come and kill those tenants, and give the vineyard to others."

When those who were listening heard this, they exclaimed, "May it never be!"

[17] But Jesus looked straight at them and said, "What then is the meaning of this passage of Scripture: 'A stone which the builders rejected has become the cornerstone'? [18] Everyone who falls upon that stone will be broken to pieces, and anyone on whom it falls will be crushed."

[19] The Scribes and Chief Priests wanted to lay their hands on him at that very moment, because they knew he had told this parable against them; but they were afraid of the people.

[20] And they kept a close eye on him by sending spies who pretended to be good men. They did this to catch him out in his teaching, so that they could hand him over to the rule and authority of the Roman Governor. [21] They asked him, "Teacher, we know that you speak and teach correctly; that

you do not show favoritism, but instead teach the way of God truthfully. [22] Is it proper for us Jews to pay a tax to Caesar, or not?"

[23] Jesus saw through their trickery and said to them, [24] "Show me a silver coin: whose image and inscription is on it?"

"Caesar's", they said.

[25] He responded, "Well then, repay to Caesar the things that are Caesar's, and to God the things that are God's". [26] They were not able to catch him out in his words in front of the people. They were amazed at his answer and became silent.

[27] Some men from the faction of the Sadducees[†]–who say there is no resurrection– came to him. [28] They asked him, "Teacher, Moses wrote for us that if a man's brother dies having a wife but no children, the man should marry his dead brother's wife and raise up children for his brother. [29] Now then, imagine there were seven brothers. The first brother married and died without children. [30] The second brother married her, [31] then the third, and so on, until all seven brothers had died and left no children. [32] Later, the woman herself died. [33] In the time of resurrection, therefore, whose wife will the woman be, since all seven men had married her?"

[34] Jesus said to them, "The people of this age[††] marry and are given in marriage, [35] but those who are counted worthy of sharing in that age and in the resurrection from the dead will not marry or be given in marriage, [36] for they can no longer die–they will be like angels. They will be God's children since they are children of the resurrection. [37] Moses also revealed that the dead will be raised in the passage about the burning bush, where he speaks about the Lord as the God of Abraham and the God of Isaac and the God of Jacob. [38] Now God is not the God of the dead but of the living; indeed all are alive to him."

[39] Some of the Scribes responded, "Teacher, you have spoken well". [40] For they no longer dared to put any questions to him.

[41] Then Jesus said to them, "How is it that they say the Christ is to be a son of King David? [42] After all, in the book of Psalms, David himself states, 'The Lord said to my lord, "Sit at my right hand [43] until I make your enemies a footstool for your feet"'. [44] Therefore, David calls the Christ 'lord'; so how can he also be David's son?"

[45] In the hearing of all the people, Jesus said to the disciples, [46] "Beware of the Scribes who like to walk about in long robes and love to be greeted by people in the markets, and to have the front seats in the synagogues and the places of honour at banquets. [47] They devour the homes of widows and pretentiously say long public prayers. They will receive more severe judgement."

Chapter 21

[1] Jesus looked up and noticed the rich dropping their gifts into the temple treasury. [2] And he saw a poor widow drop in two small coins. [3] He said, "Truly, I tell you, that this poor widow has given more than all of them. [4] For they all gave from their surplus, but she, in her poverty, gave all that she had to live on."

[5] When some were speaking about the temple, how it had been adorned with beautiful stones and offerings, he said, [6] "These stones you are looking at–days are coming when not one stone will be left on another; they will all be torn down".

[7] And they asked him, "Teacher, when will these things be, and what will be the sign when they are about to happen?"

[8] He replied, "See that you are not deceived, for many will come in my name saying 'I am he' and 'The time is near'. Do not go after them. [9] When you hear of wars and insurrections, do not panic. For these things must happen first, but the end will not follow at once."

---

† The Sadducees were a fairly secular group within Judaism, drawing mainly from the ruling class.

†† That is, this aeon, this period of time.

[10] Then he said to them, "Nation will rise against nation, and kingdom against kingdom. [11] There will be great earthquakes, and famines and plagues in various places, and terrors and great signs in the sky. [12] But before all these things, they will seize you and persecute you, handing you over to the synagogues and prisons, and bringing you before kings and governors for the sake of my name. [13] This will become a time for you to bear testimony. [14] Make up your mind, then, not to prepare your defence beforehand; [15] for I will give you speech and wisdom which none of your adversaries will be able to withstand or contradict. [16] You will be betrayed by parents and brothers and relatives and friends. They will put some of you to death, [17] and you will be hated by everyone because of my name. [18] Yet not a hair of your head will be lost. [19] Through your endurance, you will gain your lives.

[20] "But when you see Jerusalem surrounded by armies, then know that her desolation is close. [21] At that time, those in Judea must flee to the hills, and those in the city itself must get out, and those in the country must not enter it. [22] For these are days when justice is dealt out, so that all that is written in the Scriptures might be fulfilled. [23] Woe to those who are pregnant and to nursing mothers in those days, for there will be great distress in the land and Anger upon this people; [24] and they will fall by the sword and be carried off captive to all the other nations, and Jerusalem will be trampled by the nations, until the times of the nations are fulfilled.

[25] "There will be signs in the sun and moon and stars; and on earth there will be great anxiety among the nations as they become perplexed at the sound and fury of the sea. [26] People will faint from fear and foreboding of what is coming on the world; for the powers of heaven will be shaken. [27] And then you will see the Son of Man coming in a cloud with power and great glory. [28] When these things start to happen, stand up and lift your heads, for your redemption is near."

[29] And he told them a parable: "Look at the fig tree, and all the trees. [30] When they sprout leaves, you can see and know for yourselves that summer is near. [31] In the same way, when you see these things happening, know that the kingdom of God is near. [32] Truly, I tell you that this generation will not pass away until all has taken place. [33] Heaven and earth will pass away, but my words will not pass away.

[34] "Watch yourselves, so that your hearts will not be weighed down by decadence, drunkenness, and the anxieties of everyday life, and that day come upon you suddenly like a trap. [35] For it will come upon all those who live on the face of the earth. [36] But watch at all times, praying that you will have the strength to escape these things which are about to take place, and stand before the Son of Man."

[37] By day, Jesus was teaching in the temple court, but at night he went out and stayed on the Mount of Olives. [38] And all the people would rise early in the morning and come to the temple to listen to him.

Chapter 22

[1] Now the festival of the Unleavened Bread, which is known as the Passover, was approaching, [2] and the Chief Priests and the Scribes were searching for how they might do away with Jesus, for they were frightened of the people. [3] Then Satan entered Judas (who was called Iscariot and who was one of the twelve). [4] He went and made plans with the Chief Priests and the temple guards as to how he could hand Jesus over to them. [5] They were delighted and arranged to give him money. [6] He accepted this arrangement, and so began to look for a good time to hand Jesus over to them without a commotion.

[7] Now the day of the Festival of Unleavened Bread arrived, in which the Passover lamb is to be sacrificed. [8] So Jesus sent Peter and John out,

saying, "Go and prepare the Passover meal for us so that we may eat it."

[9] "Where would you like us to prepare it?" they said.

[10] He replied, "As you enter the city, a man carrying a jar of water will meet you. Follow him to the house he goes into, [11] and say to the owner of the house, 'The teacher asks you, "Where is the room in which I may eat the Passover meal with my disciples?"'. [12] And he will show you a large furnished room upstairs. Prepare things there."

[13] So they went out and found things just the way he had said, and they made preparations for the Passover meal.

[14] When the time came, Jesus reclined at the table with his apostles. [15] He said to them, "I have intensely desired to eat this Passover meal with you before I suffer. [16] For I tell you, I will not eat it again until it has reached its fulfillment in the kingdom of God."

[17] He took a cup of wine, gave thanks for it and said, "Take this and share it among yourselves. [18] For I tell you, from now on I will not drink of the fruit of the vine until the kingdom of God comes."

[19] He took a loaf of bread, gave thanks for it, broke it and gave it to them saying, "This is my body which is given for you; do this in remembrance of me".

[20] And in the same way, after eating the meal, he took the cup of wine and said, "This cup is the new covenant with my blood, which is poured out for you. [21] But see, the hand of my betrayer is with me on the table. [22] For the Son of Man is going just as it has been determined. Yet woe to that man by whom he is betrayed." [23] Then they began to discuss among themselves which one of them was about to do this.

[24] An argument arose among them as to which of them seemed to be the greatest. [25] So he said to them, "The kings of the other nations dominate their subjects, and those placed in authority over the subjects are called 'Benefactors'. [26] But it is not to be so with you. Rather, the greatest among you is to become like the youngest, and the one who leads like the one who serves. [27] For who is greater—the one who reclines at the table or the one serving the meal? It is the one who reclines at the table, is it not? Yet I myself am among you as one who serves.

[28] "You are the ones who have stood by me during my trials. [29] And just as my Father gave me kingly authority, I give the same to you, [30] so that you may eat and drink at my table in my kingdom. And you will sit upon thrones judging the twelve tribes of Israel.

[31] "Simon, Simon, listen! Satan has insisted that he sift you like wheat, [32] but I have prayed for you that your faith might not fail. And when you have turned back, strengthen your brothers."

[33] Peter said to Jesus, "Lord, I am prepared to go with you to prison and to death!"

[34] But Jesus replied, "I tell you, Peter, before the rooster crows today you will have denied knowing me three times". [35] Then he said to them, "When I sent you out without a wallet, bag or sandals, you did not lack anything did you?"

"Not a thing", they answered.

[36] He said to them, "Now, however, whoever has a wallet, take it; likewise, a bag. Whoever does not have a sword should sell his cloak and purchase one. [37] For I tell you, this piece of Scripture must be completed in my life: 'He is considered as one of the outlaws'. Indeed, this Scripture about me is even now coming to its completion."

[38] Then they said, "Lord, look, here are two swords!"

"That is enough", he replied.

The Arrest, Trial and Execution of Jesus

[39] Then Jesus left the house and made his way to the Mount of Olives, where he usually went, and the disciples followed him. [40] When they reached the place, he said to them, "Pray that you will not succumb to the time of trial". [41] And he withdrew about a stone's throw from them, knelt down and

prayed: [42] "Father, if you are willing, please take this cup away from me. Yet, may your will be done, not mine."[†]

[45] And getting up from his prayer, he returned to his disciples and found them asleep because of their grief. [46] He asked them, "Why do you sleep? Arise and pray that you will not succumb to the time of trial."

[47] While he was still speaking, a mob appeared and leading them was the man named Judas, one of the twelve. [48] He approached Jesus to kiss him, but Jesus said, "Judas, are you betraying the Son of Man with a kiss?"

[49] Seeing what was about to happen, those around him said, "Lord, should we strike with the sword?" [50] And one of them struck the Chief Priest's servant and cut off his right ear.

[51] But Jesus answered them, "Enough of this". And he touched his ear and healed him.

[52] Jesus said to those who had come to arrest him, the Chief Priests and captains of the temple guard and Elders, "Have you come with swords and clubs, as if I am a criminal? [53] I was with you daily in the temple, and you did not lay a hand on me. But this is your hour; this is the authority of darkness."

[54] Then they seized him and led him away, and took him to the Chief Priest's house. Peter followed at a distance. [55] A fire had been lit in the middle of the courtyard, and Peter sat down with those who were around it. [56] A servant girl noticed him sitting in the light, and she stared at him, and said, "This one also was with him".

[57] But Peter denied it, "Woman, I do not know him".

[58] A short time later, someone else looked at him and said, "You are one of them as well".

But Peter said, "Sir, I am not".

[59] An hour or so later, another one said quite emphatically, "In truth, this man was also with him; in fact, he is a Galilean".

[60] But Peter said, "Sir, I do not know what you are talking about". And immediately, while he was still speaking, the rooster crowed. [61] And the Lord turned and looked at Peter, and Peter remembered the Lord's prediction, how he had said to him 'Before the rooster crows today, you will deny me three times'. [62] And Peter went outside and wept bitterly.

[63] Now the men who were holding Jesus mocked him and beat him. [64] They blindfolded him and asked him, "Prophesy! Who is it who struck you?" [65] And they heaped many other insults on him.

[66] As the day broke, the Elders of the people, the Chief Priests and the Scribes gathered together, and Jesus was led out before their council.

They inquired, [67] "If you are the Christ, tell us so!"

But he replied, "If I were to tell you, you would not believe. [68] And if I were to ask you a question, you would not answer. [69] From this time on, though, the Son of Man will be seated at God's right hand of power."

[70] They all said, "So you are the Son of God?"

But he replied, "You yourselves confirm that I am".

[71] And they responded, "What more testimony do we need? We have heard it from his own mouth."

Chapter 23

[1] Then the whole lot of them rose and brought him to Governor Pilate. [2] They began to accuse him, "We found this man perverting our nation and discouraging people from paying taxes to Caesar, and saying that he himself is Christ, a king".

[3] So Pilate asked him, "Are you the king of the Jews?"

†   Some ancient manuscripts add: " [43] An angel from heaven appeared to him, and strengthened him. [44] And being in great distress, he prayed all the more earnestly, and his sweat was like drops of blood falling to the ground."

Jesus answered, "Do you yourself say so?"[†]

[4] Pilate said to the Chief Priests and the crowds, "I can find no fault with this man".

[5] But they grew more insistent. "He is stirring up the people, teaching throughout the whole of Judea, starting in Galilee and ending up here."

[6] When Pilate heard this, he asked whether the man was from Galilee. [7] And when he discovered that Jesus was under Herod's jurisdiction, he sent him to Herod, who was himself in Jerusalem at that time.

[8] Now when Herod saw Jesus he was overjoyed. He had been wanting to see Jesus for some time, because he had heard about him, and hoped to see him perform some miraculous sign. [9] He questioned him at length, but Jesus said nothing in reply.

[10] The Chief Priests and the Scribes stood there, vehemently accusing him. [11] And Herod held Jesus in contempt, and with the help of his soldiers, he ridiculed him, dressed him in fancy clothes, and sent him back to Pilate. [12] (On that day, Herod and Pilate became friends with each other; for previously there had been hostility between them.)

[13] Pilate called together the Chief Priests, the leaders and the people, [14] and said to them, "You brought this man to me as one who was perverting the people. I interrogated him in your presence, but found no cause for any of your accusations against him. [15] Moreover, neither did Herod, for he sent him back to us. And indeed he has done nothing deserving of death. [16] Therefore, I will order a flogging, and then release him."[††]

[18] But they cried out together, "Take him away! Release Barabbas to us!" [19] (Barabbas was in prison for an insurrection that had occurred in the city, and for murder).

[20] Pilate wanted to release Jesus, and so he spoke to them again. [21] But they cried out, "Crucify! Crucify him!"

[22] A third time, Pilate said to them, "For what? Has he done anything evil? I have found no grounds for the death penalty in this man. Therefore, I will order a flogging, and then release him."

[23] But the crowd kept demanding with loud voices that he be crucified; and their voices won the day. [24] Pilate decided to grant their request. [25] He released the man who had been imprisoned for insurrection and murder—as they requested—and gave Jesus up to what they wanted.

[26] And as they led him away, they seized a man named Simon (from Cyrene) who was coming in from the country. They laid the cross on him, and made him carry it behind Jesus.

[27] Now a great crowd of people followed him, including women who were mourning and wailing for him. [28] Jesus turned to them and said, "Daughters of Jerusalem, do not weep over me; but weep for yourselves and for your children. [29] For days are coming when they will say, 'Blessed are the barren women, and the wombs which have born no children, and the breasts which have fed none'. [30] At that time, they will say to the mountains, 'Fall on us' and to the hills, 'Cover us'. [31] For if this is what they do when the tree is green, what will happen when it is withered?"

[32] Two others who were criminals were also led with him to be executed. [33] And when they arrived at the place called 'The Skull', they crucified him there along with the criminals—one on Jesus' right, the other on his left. [34†] And the soldiers divided his clothing by placing bets; [35] and the people stood by watching.

The leaders even made fun of him, saying, "He rescued others, let him rescue himself if he really is God's Christ, his Chosen One".

[36] The soldiers also ridiculed him. Approaching him, they offered him bitter wine, [37] and said, "If you really are the King of the Jews, rescue your-

---

† Or *you say that I am.*

†† Some ancient manuscripts add: "[17] On account of the festival, he was obliged to release one man to them."

† Some ancient manuscripts add: "And Jesus said, 'Father, forgive them, for they do not know what they are doing.'"

self". [38] There was a placard above him which read: THIS IS THE KING OF THE JEWS.

[39] One of the criminals who hung there was abusing Jesus, saying, "Aren't you supposed to be the Christ? Rescue yourself and us".

[40] But the other criminal responded with a rebuke: "Have you no fear of God? After all, you are under the same death sentence. [41] Yet, we are here justly; we are receiving what we deserve for our actions, but he has done nothing wrong."

[42] Then he said, "Jesus, please remember me when you come into your kingdom".

[43] And Jesus replied, "I tell you the truth, today you will be with me in Paradise".

[44] By this time, it was already about midday. Darkness came over the whole land until three in the afternoon, [45] because the sun stopped shining. The curtain of the Temple was torn down the middle. [46] Then Jesus cried out in a loud voice, "Father, into your hands I entrust my spirit!" With these words he breathed his last breath.

[47] When the centurion saw what happened he praised God, saying, "This was truly a righteous man". [48] When the crowd that had gathered for this spectacle saw these things, they beat their chests and returned to their homes. [49] But all Jesus' acquaintances and the women who had followed him from Galilee stood at a distance watching these things.

[50] Now there was a man named Joseph who was a member of the Council. He was a good and just man [51] and had not given his consent to their decision and action. He came from the Jewish town of Arimathea and was waiting expectantly for God's kingdom. [52] He went to Pilate and asked for the body of Jesus. [53] And when he had taken it down from the cross, he wrapped it in linen and placed it in a tomb cut out from rock, in which no-one had ever been laid.

[54] It was the Day of Preparation, and the Sabbath was drawing near, [55] but still the women who had accompanied Jesus from Galilee, followed Joseph and took note of the tomb and how Jesus' body was laid there. [56] Returning home they prepared some burial perfumes and lotions. But on the Sabbath Day they rested according to the commandment.

Chapter 24

The Resurrection and Appearances of Jesus

[1] Now, very early on Sunday morning, the women went to the tomb with the burial lotions they had prepared. [2] They found the stone-door rolled away from the tomb, [3] but when they went in they did not find the body of the Lord Jesus. [4] And as they stood there perplexed about this, suddenly two men in gleaming clothes approached them. [5] Terrified, the women bowed down with their faces to the ground, and the men said to them, "Why do you search among the dead for someone who is alive? [6] He is not here; rather he has been raised! Remember how he told you while he was still in Galilee, [7] 'The Son of Man must be betrayed into the hands of sinful people and be crucified, and on the third day be raised up'." [8] And they remembered his words.

[9] Returning from the tomb, the women told all these things to the eleven apostles and all the other people there. [10] (The women were Mary Magdalene, Joanna, Mary the mother of James, and some others with them.) [11] Yet the apostles did not believe them because these reports seemed like nonsense to them.

[12] All the same, Peter got up and ran to the tomb. Bending over, he saw the burial clothes lying by themselves. He returned home amazed at what had happened.

[13] Now that same day, two of them were travelling to a town about eleven kilometres† from Jerusalem, called Emmaus. [14] They were talking with each other about all that had happened. [15] While they were talking and discussing, Jesus

† Literally, *sixty stadia*.

himself approached them and began to walk alongside them, [16] but their eyes were kept from recognising him.

[17] He asked them, "What are these things you are discussing with each other as you walk along?" They stood there depressed, [18] and one of them, whose name was Cleopas, asked, "Are you the only visitor to Jerusalem who does not know about the events that have taken place there in these days?"

[19] "What events?" he asked.

They replied, "The events surrounding Jesus of Nazareth, who was a prophet powerful in word and deed before God and all the people, [20] and how the Chief Priests and our leaders handed him over to a death sentence and crucified him. [21] We were hoping that he was the one who was going to redeem Israel. But on top of all this, it is now the third day since all these things happened. [22] And then to add to it, some women from our group surprised us. They were at the tomb early this morning, [23] and when they didn't find the body they came saying that they had seen a vision of angels, who said he was alive. [24] And some of those with us went back to the tomb and found it exactly as the women described, but they did not see him."

[25] And Jesus said to them, "You are so foolish, and slow of heart to believe all the things the Prophets foretold! [26] Didn't the Christ have to suffer these things and so enter his glory?" [27] And beginning with the writings of Moses and all the prophets, he explained to them the things written about himself in all the Scriptures.

[28] They approached the town where they were going and Jesus gave the impression he was going further on. [29] But they urged him, "Stay with us because it is evening; the day is already over".

So he went in to stay with them. [30] When he was reclining at the table with them, he took the loaf of bread, gave thanks, broke it and gave it to them. [31] Then their eyes were opened and they recognized him, but he disappeared from their sight. [32] They said to one another, "Were not our hearts on fire as he spoke to us on the road and explained the Scriptures to us?"

[33] They got up straight away and returned to Jerusalem, where they found the eleven apostles and those with them gathered together, [34] who said, "The Lord really has been raised to life, and he has appeared to Simon". [35] Then the two related the things that had happened on the road, and how they had recognized him when he broke the loaf of bread.

[36] While they were talking about these things, Jesus stood right in the middle of them and said, "Peace to you". [37] Thinking they were seeing a spirit, they were startled and terrified.

[38] But Jesus said to them, "Why are you disturbed and why do doubts arise in your hearts? [39] Look at my hands and feet, for it really is me. Touch me and see, for a spirit does not have flesh and bones, as you can see I have." [40] He said this, and showed them his hands and feet. [41] But when they still did not believe because of joy and amazement, he said to them, "Do you have anything here I can eat?" [42] So they handed him a piece of cooked fish. [43] He took it and ate it right in front of them.

[44] Then he said to them, "I told you about these things while I was still with you: everything that is written about me in the Law of Moses, the Prophets and the Psalms had to be fulfilled". [45] Then he opened their minds to understand the Scriptures [46] and said, "This is what is written: the Christ will suffer and rise from the dead on the third day, [47] and in his name repentance for the forgiveness of sins will be announced to all nations, beginning from Jerusalem.

[48] "You are witnesses of these things, [49] and so I will send to you the promise of my Father. You yourselves stay here in the city until you are clothed with power from heaven."

[50] Then he led them out to Bethany. He raised his hands and blessed them. [51] As he was blessing them, he departed from them and was taken up into heaven. [52] They worshipped him and then returned to Jerusalem with great joy, [53] where they were always in the temple court, praising God.

This Feedback Form appears in each Guest's Manual. Please encourage your guests to fill it in after you have completed the course and give it to you. You may wish to talk it through before people fill it out.

Name: _____

Why did you decide to do the *Simply Christianity* course?

_____

_____

If you can remember, what were your expectations, hesitations, hopes, worries, etc., about attending *Simply Christianity* before you came to the first meeting?

_____

_____

Was the number of weeks given to the course appropriate? If not, how many weeks do you think would make the course more attractive?

_____

_____

How would you have described your Christian knowledge and commitment prior to coming to the *Simply Christianity* course?

_____

_____

In what way(s) has the course helped your Christian knowledge or commitment? (Please be specific.)

_____

_____

Would you say that you are a 'Christian' (someone who has experienced repentance and forgiveness)? Why/why not?

_____

_____

Was the amount of reading 'at home' each week reasonable given how busy we all are?

_____

_____

Was the time given each night to answering questions an appropriate length?

_____

_____

Do you have still unanswered questions which you had hoped would be covered over the five weeks?

_____

_____

_____

What were the best things about the course?

_____

_____

_____

In what ways could the course be improved for future groups?

_____

_____

_____

Are you interested in further small group Bible study?

_____

_____

Any other comments?

_____

_____

_____

_____

_____

_____

Please return this form to me as soon as is convenient.

Fax:

Post: Thank you.

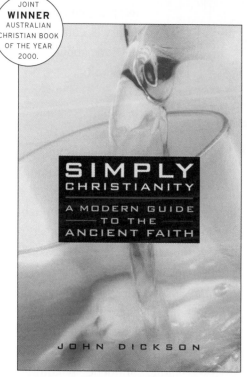